Mickey:
The Giveaway Boy

By Robert M. Shafer

Edited by Barbara Lockwood

Published in North America and Europe by Running Wild Press. Visit Running Wild Press at www.runningwildpress.com Educators, librarians, book clubs (as well as the eternally curious), go to www.runningwildpress.com for teaching tools.

ISBN (pbk) 978-1-947041-31-8
ISBN (ebook) 978-1-947041-35-6

Neither slavery nor involuntary servitude, except as a punishment for crime whereof the party shall have been duly convicted, shall exist within the United States, or any place subject to their jurisdiction.

Constitution of the United States of America – Amendment XIII

Chapter 1

I'd just celebrated my ninth birthday with Mom and my two older brothers, Tommy and Ben, when Mom announced she was giving me away. Again.

I stood at the kitchen window watching it rain. Not a downpour to wash away the filth, it was a depressing drizzle that turned coal dust and chimney smoke into muck that clung to every factory, warehouse, and tenement within sight. The dampness magnified Chicago's stench of manufacturing, uncollected garbage, and traffic exhaust.

"Your soup is almost ready, Mickey."

"Thanks, Mom."

A cigarette dangled from her mouth. She banged the spoon against the sides of the pan as she heated my soup on the small kerosene stove. The ash at the tip of her Camel was growing too long, and I hoped it wouldn't fall in my supper. It was rare for Mom to be careless. She liked clean and neat no matter how poor our living conditions were.

The leaky stove vent spit out soot that coated the windows, walls, and ceiling. I rubbed my shirtsleeve against the glass pane to remove enough grime I could see further out the window. A low-hanging gray sky hid the tops of downtown Chicago's taller buildings. Despite the shabby neighborhood and rundown building, we lived in, I was really happy to be back with my mother and my two brothers for the last year.

Tommy hadn't been home for a couple of weeks. He believed he was too old and tough to hang around with Ben and me anymore.

"Where is he? So many awful things could happen to him."

"Don't worry, Mom," I said. "He'll come home."

Ben and I knew our brother wasn't far away.

Tommy liked his weird friend more than his family; they spent every minute together. The guy was at least sixteen, four years older than Tommy. I wondered what bad stuff they were up to.

Tommy warned Ben and me he'd punch us square in the face if we told Mom about his friend or where he hung out. He didn't care if he hurt her feelings. He took pleasure in it. I couldn't do that. She always made me feel guilty about not being there when she needed me. Lately, she complained a lot about being lonely.

"I'm here, Mom," Ben said. "Who cares if Tommy ever comes home?"

"Don't talk about Tommy that way, Ben."

"I'll take care of you, Mom," Ben promised.

I kept my mouth shut. I worried she cared about Tommy the most, and the same thought drove Ben crazy.

Ben gave her a defiant look, pushed his chair over as he stood up and stomped out of the apartment slamming the door shut behind him.

I picked up the chair and slid it neatly back in place. Now, it was just the two of us, and her presence made even this dump brighter and warmer. Stealing, fighting, and skipping school were part of being with Tommy and Ben. It was hard to know things were bad, until after I did them. I felt pretty low rolling drunks on skid row, and cheating perverts out of money. Now, my brothers went their separate ways and left me behind. I hated being alone on the streets. If I had a choice, I'd rather have Mom all to myself. It hadn't seemed so dangerous when I was younger.

"Here's your soup, Mickey."

Mom put my bowl of soup on the table. I stared at it. It looked like a bowl full of blood. Jesus Christ. She forgot how much I hate tomato soup. With the mood she was in, I wasn't going to complain. Since my brothers were out, I could eat at a comfortable speed and not worry about them spitting in my food. I could have all the saltine crackers I wanted to help the soup down.

"I'm sorry, Mickey. Tomato soup is all we have right now."

Wow. She did remember I hate it. "That's okay, Mom."

She sat down across from me and let out an exaggerated sigh. As usual, she clutched her cup of coffee with one hand and managed her cigarette with the other.

"Mickey," she said. "I talked to a woman on the phone. We talked about you."

I looked up so fast I spilled soup on my overalls.

"Why? What about me, Mom?

"About you living with her and her husband."

"I don't want to live with other people again, Mom." My voice rose to a screech when I felt panic. I hate sounding that way. I put my spoon down and looked at the red glob on my pant leg. At least it wasn't on my crotch. I tried to rub the stain away with my hand, and I kept looking up and down. I didn't want to miss the expression on Mom's face, in case she said more of those horrible words.

"I can't take proper care of you right now." She talked off into the distance as if I was somewhere else. Damn you, Mom, look at me.

"You take great care of me, Mom." I heard the sissy fear in my voice.

"You'll have a clean place to sleep, Mickey. It'll be a place without rats running around everywhere."

"I don't mind the rats, Mom." What a huge lie. I was terrified of the stinking rats.

Her eyes settled on me for a couple of seconds and then moved on. "You'll have enough food to eat."

"I have enough food, Mom. See. I'm eating my soup. I'm getting full." I grabbed two more saltine crackers and stuffed them in my mouth.

She took her hand from her coffee cup and pushed her hair back from her forehead. She did her best I'm-so-tired act, again.

"Of course, you're hungry, Mickey. You boys are always hungry."

That was only partly true. We stole lots of good stuff to eat. We stole so much candy we got sick eating it. If we hustled enough money, we feasted on tamales from the carts downtown and in the lakefront parks. Those steaming hot tamales were delicious. Ben complained the most. Why didn't he keep his big mouth shut? This "living with other people" crap was happening to me again because of his constant whining. He couldn't shut up about our lousy food, the rat hole we lived in, how he wanted to go out to California to find Dad and how he wanted to visit Dad's family in Indiana. Dad's family didn't care one bit about us anymore. They didn't want anything to do with what was left of our family after Dad took off for California with Baby John.

"You and I are going to visit Naomi tomorrow."

"Who's Naomi?"

"The woman I talked to on the phone."

"What's she like?"

"She sounded really nice."

"What about Tommy and Ben?" My voice came out scared and whiny no matter how tough I tried to sound. "Do they get to stay with you?"

She stubbed her cigarette out in the ashtray, glanced at me for a second and turned away to speak to that distant person. She looked like she might cry. Jesus Christ. I felt sorrier for her than I did for myself. I hated how she did that.

"I haven't figured that out yet, Mickey. I just don't know what else to do."

I couldn't think of anything to say. I remembered how she left Steve with Doris and me with Rose and George and how much that hurt. Jesus. She couldn't abandon me again. She couldn't.

She stood abruptly and went to her room to get ready for work. I ate most of my damn tomato soup but barely tasted it. I took my dish to the sink and did my best job of washing it. That would impress her.

Was it just me Mom didn't want to own anymore? What had I done to cause her not to love me? Why did she talk me into leaving Rose and George? They wanted to adopt me, but Mom begged me to come back home with her. That was only a year ago, and now she wanted to give me away again.

When she visited me on Christmas day, she said she wanted me to come back home with her because she loved me so much. She promised we'd be together forever. I thought she'd cry if I didn't come home. I hate remembering how mad Rose had been because I wanted to leave her and George. They'd been generous and kind to me, and I was terribly ungrateful. I made Rose cry. No matter what choices I made, I always upset someone.

Two years ago, when Doris had a choice of keeping Ben, Steve or me, I hoped to be picked, but Steve won because he was the youngest. When someone chose which kid to keep, it really paid off to be the youngest. I wondered what Steve was doing right now, at this very moment. He was lucky to live with a rich woman like Doris. I tried to picture Steve in my mind, but he stayed blurry. Mom never mentioned him anymore.

Mom came back into the kitchen holding a newly lit cigarette. Her red and white-checkered waitress uniform showed her legs from the knee down. With her hair pinned up neatly and her makeup perfect, she looked like a movie actress. I inhaled her perfume smell and felt her softness as she gave me a hug and a noisy kiss on my cheek. I was sure she'd left lipstick on me, and I didn't like that.

"I love you, Mickey." She glanced down at me. Foolishly, I still wanted to marry her, so she couldn't ever give me away again. "There's bologna in the icebox for later. Be sure to leave some for Ben."

I couldn't find any words to say. I didn't want her to hear tears welling up in my voice. The door closed behind her, and I listened to her footsteps fade away.

Mom's shift at the restaurant lasted from five in the evening until two in the morning. Many times, she didn't come home right after work. If Ben didn't show up, I was on my own for most of the night. I was too afraid to go out on the streets by myself. Damn. Why had everyone deserted me? Not a damn thing was going right.

I searched the apartment for ghosts. I searched behind the doors, in the closets and under the beds. I didn't find any, but I still worried. Outside the kitchen window, city lights and dark shadows replaced daylight. Jesus! It was black and scary nighttime, and I only had my frightened self for company. I jumped at every sound that came from inside the walls, behind the icebox, and under the sink. There were creaks and groans from overhead and the hallway outside our door. Fire truck sirens, distant shouts of anger and cries of babies all signaled danger on the prowl.

I listened to mice running in the walls. It sounded like hundreds of them. I imagined mouse heads popping out from holes in the walls, gnawed by their sharp little teeth. Swarms of nasty little rodents could crawl up my pant legs to attack my privates. I didn't want to think about the rats. With their huge yellow teeth, they could chew this whole building into a pile of rubble.

Quiet scared me as much as the noises. I wolfed down six slices of bologna and drank ice-cold water directly from the faucet. There were five slices left for Ben; if he wasn't satisfied with that, the hell with him. I needed to piss, and there was no way I was going out in the hallway to the community toilet. I pulled a chair over to the kitchen sink and climbed up. With the faucet on full, I pissed into the stream of water. I shook off and dribbled on my pant leg. Thankfully, there wasn't anyone to point out the stains and laugh at me.

I escaped to the bedroom, shed my clothes, hid under the covers and shivered, curled as tight as a spooked pill bug. I covered my ears with my hands. I feared the whole outside world and dreaded the nightmares that came with sleep.

Ben came home, stomped into our room, turned on the ceiling light, and slammed our bedroom door behind him. I couldn't make myself wake up and warn him Mom was back to getting rid of us. At least, she planned to get rid of me. I sensed his anger as he stood over me. I was sure he wanted to swear at me and punch me really hard, but he must have been tired because he left me alone. He turned off the overhead light and settled for the pallet on the floor. I was glad to be in the bed, above the rats that prowled in the night. When I slept alone in our room, I worried those rodents with their long toenails and sharp teeth would crawl up the side of the bed and bite me to death. Since Ben was on the floor, they'd attack him first. Hopefully, he'd be all they wanted to eat.

Ben and Mom arguing woke me in the morning.

"You love him more than you love me," Ben hurled the old accusation at her.

"I love all of you, Benny. Mickey and I have to make this trip today."

Damn. If he knew the awful thing about to happen to me, he wouldn't be so eager to take my place. I'd be glad to have him come along. This Naomi woman might want to give him a home instead of me.

"I'm sick of being alone," Ben said. "You never spend any time with me, Mom."

I walked into the kitchen. I was barely awake and needed to piss. Ben scowled at me.

"Good morning, Mickey." Mom greeted me with a forced smile. It was easy to see she was in a bad mood.

"Good morning, Mom. I have to go out to the toilet."

We shared the hallway bathroom with the building's other tenants. I thanked God it wasn't being used at the moment, but somebody had just shit a big one and hadn't flushed. I figured Ben had done that nasty dump and hoped I'd find it. I tried not to breathe while I stood in there. I wasn't going to flush the damn thing either. It might overflow and foul my feet before I could escape.

When I went back in the apartment, Mom and Ben were still arguing. He gave me a dirty look. He slammed the door as he huffed out of our apartment. She was grouchy about getting up early for this awful trip and for the way Ben behaved. As usual, I wanted to please everyone, and I was the one in terrible danger.

Chapter 2

Mom and I made the westward trip from our North Side tenement neighborhood by way of the Lake Street elevated train. Rather than sit together, Mom took an aisle seat next to an old woman and sent me to a window seat across from her. I had to squeeze by a wheezy, fat man in a shabby, brown suit. He was reading a newspaper and looked daggers at me for bumping into one of his big feet. He acted like I damaged his worn and scuffed shoe. The idiot didn't move one inch so I could get by him.

Usually, a ride on the elevated train excited me. Hundreds of billboards and signs on the sides of buildings sped past like a movie flickers across a theater screen. No building wall along the elevated was left undecorated. There were advertisements for hundreds of nice things like wristwatches and refrigerators my family couldn't afford to buy and wouldn't ever have. I never saw people on the street who were as handsome and perfect as those on the billboards. If I ever did, I'm sure they wouldn't want to be close to a ragged, slum kid like me.

The train whizzed so close past buildings, I could see through windows into people's apartments. Not a lot happened inside those places this time of the day. Most of the renters had rushed off to work or school. In the hot summertime, I'd seen half-naked kids with their asses and weenies showing. Muscular, hairy men in dirty tee shirts sat at small tables in their kitchens and bellowed at their kids. Sweaty-browed mothers in loose-fitting housedresses served steaming plates of cabbage or boiled potatoes or their favorite home country food. The fat man next to me smelled like sauerkraut; I hated sauerkraut. Fatso took more than his share of the seat and squeezed me against the train window. At times, I really hated grownups.

As the train hurtled on, I leaned with the sharp curves and covered my ears to dull the sound of screeching metal wheels on metal rails. Flocks of spooked pigeons took to the air as the noisy cars roared past their gathering places. Those pests flew from every crevice, leaving piles of pigeon shit on the metal under-structure of the Elevated.

The train chattered to a stop at a station and filled with red-faced, miserable looking men in hot, itchy wool suits, grey-haired, old ladies clutching worn purses to their sagging chests, and heavy-bodied immigrant women off to work in dusty factories or to scrub rich people's toilets. I was proud my mother didn't look like them and didn't have to scrub floors on her hands and knees. Working as a waitress and rushing around a crowded, noisy restaurant was a glamorous and fun job.

Laborers in grease-stained, overalls carried lunch pails in their calloused hands. I looked for hands with missing fingers. How horrible it must be to see your own finger cut from your hand and your blood spurting everywhere. People would scream and run away. It'd hurt like hell, and you'd have missing fingers the rest of your life.

The Elevated wasn't much fun for me today. Not even seeing hunchbacks, dwarfs or cripples struggle down the train aisles would cheer me up. I was on my way to meet a stranger Mom said I might have to live with. I struggled with that frightening thought. I tried to create a picture of what could happen to me. It was terrifying to imagine once again being separated from my family. When would I see Tommy and Ben again? Surely, it would be within a few hours after the visit with this woman was over. Mom wouldn't really leave me with a stranger again. We had so many relatives in Mom's family. Grandma Goldie or one of my uncles or aunts might want me to live with them. Why couldn't I stay with someone I knew until Mom had enough money to take me back and keep me forever?

I pressed my face against the train window. The jerks and bumps made my face bounce against the glass and its metal frame. It hurt, but I didn't care. If I injured myself and bled lots of blood, Mom would feel sorry for me. Then, she couldn't possibly leave me with this Naomi woman. If I pushed hard enough, I could disappear through the glass. I'd magically escape into a world filled with tons of delicious spaghetti with meatballs, chocolate cake, and strawberry ice cream. I'd have my own room filled with the world's best toys, and I'd own a beautiful, red bicycle. That was the kind of life I had with Rose and George. But I was stupid enough to leave them and go back home with Mom. Jesus Christ. What an idiot I am.

Across the aisle, Mom was taking a nap. The window seat next to her was empty. Both Mister Sauerkraut and the old woman had gotten off the train. I slipped over next to Mom, being careful not to step on her feet. She barely noticed me, but I was glad to be close to her again.

Outside the window, a sign said we were passing through Garfield Park. I was impressed by a huge, block long and block wide, mostly glass building crowded with hundreds of trees, bushes, and colorful flowers. I hadn't ever seen a building with so much glass. I thought it would be great fun to throw rocks through all that glass, but of course, I didn't do destructive things like that anymore. Mom was awake and lit a cigarette.

"What's that building, Mom?" I said "Mom" as lovingly as I could.

"That's the Garfield Conservatory, Mickey." She blew out a stream of smoke.

"Wow. That's a huge glass building, Mom." I wanted her and me to be the best of friends again.

"That's a greenhouse, Mickey. It's one of the largest greenhouses in the world," she said. "I've been inside it."

I felt really encouraged by her offering more than the shortest answer to my question.

"You'll live close to a wonderful park, Mickey. It has a lovely lake, and people can rent rowboats to go out on the water."

"Wow. You and I could visit it together, Mom. We could go out in a rowboat, and I'd do all the rowing."

She didn't answer me. I couldn't think of anything else to say. She puffed deeply on her cigarette and went back into herself.

I glanced at the passing scenery, then back at her.

She dropped her cigarette butt on the floor and crushed it with her shoe. She took out her compact. She clicked the latch on the front and the compact popped open, releasing the sweet smell of face powder. She held the compact close to her face and dabbed a bit of powder on her cheekbones. She looked carefully at her reflection in the powder-flecked mirror. She didn't like what she saw. She dug through her purse and came out with her lipstick. She pursed her lips as she looked into the mirror and applied a small amount from the red stick. She popped her lips apart and studied her appearance in the mirror.

I knew her act! She didn't want to look too cheerful in front of me or chat with me. This wasn't a train ride for us to have fun. It was a business trip. It was a trip to get rid of me. I knew what she was up to!

She took a small bottle from her purse. She dabbed a bit of perfume behind each of her ears and at the hollow of her neck.

She put all her woman stuff back into her purse and snapped the latch closed. Most of the womanly smells were locked inside her purse, but the scents floating off her intoxicated me. I loved her, and I hated her. Usually, she was smiley, full of hugs and completely lovey-dovey. If she were ugly and screechy like a witch, it wouldn't hurt me so much to be abandoned by her.

We jerked to a stop at the station right after Garfield Park.

"This is where we get off, Mickey."

She stood up. I hung onto the back of her jacket as we squeezed our way off the train. Adults pressed against me and someone stepped on my foot. I was pushed against a man with a huge belly and stinky body odor. I hated being crowded against people who were so tall I barely reached past their middles. I hated their bad smells and their farts right in my face. We broke free of the mass of people, and I gulped a breath of cleaner air.

The train refilled, screeched, and rumbled off as Mom and I made our way through the exit turnstile.

Two flights of stairs descended from the green-painted El station. The walls were covered with handbills and posters layered on every flat surface. There were advertisements for bottles of Coca-Cola, packs of Camel cigarettes, Brylcreem hair lotion, Max Factor lipstick, and downtown theatre musicals. I enjoyed looking at the colorful pictures, especially the camel, the pyramids and the palm trees on the cigarette package. I liked the pretty women holding the lipstick tubes close to their bright-red lips.

We walked past a poster that showed Uncle Sam pointing his finger directly at people. He said, "I want you for the U. S. Army." I wondered if Uncle Sam would ever want someone like me for the U.S. Army. Would I ever be tall enough, strong enough and brave enough to be a soldier?

I usually bounced happily down the stairs from a train station. Today, I forced myself to walk down the steps. I had no idea what Mom planned to do. I thought I was a tough nine-year-old when I had my two older brothers close by to help me. Right now, I didn't feel tough at all. I was terribly frightened.

From the elevated station at Lake Street and Hamlin Avenue, it was a long eight-block walk to the woman's house. The neighborhood looked a lot better than the slum we lived in. Most of the buildings were two-story brick houses with front porches. Trees and small lawns separated them from the sidewalk and street. Several had side yards with flower and vegetable gardens.

I needed to break into a run to keep up with Mom's long, quick stride. She was in a big hurry to get rid of me.

"The name of the woman I talked to is Naomi," she reminded me. "This could work out well for you, Mickey."

"I want to stay with you and Tommy and Ben," I whined. "Please, Mom." I hated the way I begged, but I was too frightened to act tough and appear like I didn't care.

She hurried on without answering me.

"This is it," she said as she checked the address with a slip of paper she took out of her purse. "This place looks real nice."

We walked up concrete steps to the house's front porch. Mom rang the doorbell. I didn't even try to push past her to ring this doorbell like I usually did.

I heard heavy footsteps approach from inside the house. When Naomi opened her front door, and I saw her for the first time, my stomach flipped over. "What a beast," my oldest brother Tommy would've said. She offered no smile or friendliness as she invited us in. A tall, heavy woman, her flabby arms ended in big hands with thick fingers. She was fat, but it looked like powerful fat. She reminded me of the movies I'd watched where the huge wife beat the hell out of her runty husband. Naomi looked like she could make a big fist and hit really hard.

Chapter 3

Mom and I sat across from Naomi in her living room filled with fancy furniture. Naomi's couches and chairs were large and covered with thick, flower and vine patterned material. At the movies, I'd seen furniture like hers in the mansions of rich people. Naomi owned lots of fine, china bric-a-brac decorated with gold gilding and colorful raised flowers. Her fancy stuff sat on doily-protected wood tables of many sizes. Photographs and paintings with elaborate silver frames hung on her walls.

Naomi wore a loose-fitting housedress and parlor slippers. The flowery material of her dress was faded, and there were little holes where the seams came together. Her slippers were run down at the sides and heels. Dark, bulky nylons hid most of her heavy legs. She looked like a person who'd scrub floors for rich people. That was it. She looked exactly like a scrubwoman. She sat in a sloppy way with her legs spread apart. I saw a bruised, blue-veined roll of flab where the nylons ended under her dress. I averted my eyes from that ugly sight.

Her face was a hard square. A blackish mole with a couple of hairs growing out of it sat in the corner of her thin-lipped mouth. She sprouted a noticeable mustache. I hadn't seen her smile since Mom and I'd arrived. Not one tiny bit of sparkle showed in her eyes. Her eyes reminded me of the eyes of a snarling, mongrel dog you needed to throw rocks at or run like hell to escape from.

I looked closely at my mother. Mom was an elegant and magical lady who always looked perfectly dressed and neat. Even if her clothes weren't the most fancy, and didn't cost a lot of money, she always looked glamorous in them. She never looked raggedy like her sons did. Naomi flashed expensive looking gold and diamond rings on her fat fingers. Mom should own rings like that. Those rings belonged on the fingers of a young, pretty woman.

"Is it okay if I smoke?" Mom asked.

"Go ahead," Naomi replied with a frown.

Mom took her Camel cigarettes and a book of matches out of her purse. She struck a match and lit her cigarette.

I looked more closely at Naomi to figure out how mean she might be. Meanness was the first thing I always looked for in grownups. Then, I figured how to stay out of their way. Naomi saw me staring and glared back at me like she wanted to slap me. I looked away. She seemed much worse than just mean.

Mom turned her head away from Naomi and me and blew out a thin stream of smoke that turned into a larger cloud and slowly dissipated. She smoked like an actress in the movies or the pretty models on billboards. An ashtray shaped like a big leaf sat on the highly-polished coffee table that separated us from Naomi. Mom expertly tapped the ash from the tip of her cigarette into it. I loved how precise she was when she smoked. Soon, I'd be old enough to smoke cigarettes, and from watching Mom, I already knew how. Still, I felt anxious about my future, and my leg twitched. My foot bumped against Naomi's coffee table.

"Don't kick the furniture," Naomi growled at me.

"Sorry," Mom said. She turned to me. "Try to sit still, Mickey." She brushed my hair back from my forehead. I twisted away from her, even though I loved the feel of her hand on my skin. "He has so much energy."

Naomi gave me a look of disapproval.

I hoped Mom saw Naomi's nasty looks at me, but she didn't appear to notice. I slumped back on the couch. I hated to sit still. I hated this fancy furniture I had to be so careful with.

"I'm looking for the best home I can find for Mickey," Mom said.

"He'll have plenty to eat and a comfortable room to himself," Naomi said.

"I can't work full time as a waitress and take proper care of my three rambunctious boys." Mom turned to me and patted my knee as if I understood how difficult her life was, and I'd accept her leaving me with this woman. I wanted to cry out to her, but she turned back to Naomi like she also wanted confirmation of her tough life from that scary woman.

"I guess that's a challenge," Naomi replied without a trace of sympathy.

"I'll send you ten dollars every week," Mom promised.

"Are you sure you can send ten dollars every week?" Naomi asked. She sounded like a copper who didn't believe anyone ever told the truth.

"Oh yes, I will. I never go back on my word."

"I hope so. I'm not offering charity." Naomi's voice grew harsh and her body puffed up to be even bigger, and her expression turned nastier.

Why did Naomi doubt my mother? Mom wasn't a liar. She didn't even get mad at the rude way Naomi talked to her. When Naomi wasn't looking at me, I gave her my nastiest frown.

"You have a lovely house," Mom said. "And you have such high-quality furniture."

"Yes, I know. I'm not rich, though. I have to be careful with my money. I have to count every penny."

"Naomi has two dogs, honey," Mom turned and smiled at me. "Won't that be fun?"

"I guess." I didn't smile back. I liked dogs, but I didn't like this Naomi woman.

I fidgeted and accidentally banged my foot against the bottom of Naomi's couch. She gave me another warning look. Mom was used to the constant movement of her boys and ignored our rough ways.

Suddenly, Mom stood up. So, did I. Naomi needed to use both of her hands and arms to push herself up from the chair. I felt sorry for the chair. At least I wouldn't be forced to see up her dress anymore.

"Well, I have to leave now, Mickey. Give me a big hug."

What the hell did Mom just say? I must have totally misunderstood her. "I'm not going with you, Mom?"

"Not right now."

"I have to stay here?" Panic gripped me. "You're not leaving me here, are you Mom?"

"I'll be back for you tomorrow, Mickey. We'll go to lunch, together. We'll see how you like it here with Naomi."

Mom couldn't possibly leave me here. She couldn't be serious. "I want to go home with you now, Mom," I pleaded. I sounded like a whiny baby, but I couldn't control how scared I was.

"You'll be fine here with Naomi. Give me a kiss."

I didn't know what to say or what move to make. Mom bent over and hugged me, but I couldn't feel anything. My face was numb to her kiss. I wanted to grab onto her, but I couldn't move my arms. What the hell was she doing to me? She was supposed to be my best friend in the world.

"He'll be okay," Naomi said.

"I love you, Mickey." Mom smiled, and her hand rested on my shoulder. Why the hell did she smile? I hadn't been able to smile at all since we'd arrived at this house. I felt sick to my stomach. I wanted to puke.

Naomi stepped between Mom and me and walked Mom to the front door blocking her from my sight. I stood there holding back my tears. I waved weakly at Mom. She didn't turn back to look at me. She didn't try to see around Naomi. She didn't wave goodbye to me.

"Please, Mom!" I meant to yell to Mom, but it came out as a tiny, little squeak. My throat was parched. My voice wouldn't work.

The front door closed behind Mom, and she was gone. Naomi turned around gave me a smug look of victory.

Chapter 4

What the hell was wrong with me? Why didn't I run after Mom and escape from this Naomi woman? I was so stupid! I stood there like a dummy, and now it was too late. Mom was gone, and she left me behind with this awful person. I didn't need to stay overnight with the beast to know I already hated it here.

A scowling Naomi walked towards me. The floor creaked under her weight. "Come into the kitchen," she ordered. Jesus, she was huge. As I obediently followed her, my legs felt like Jell-O, and my stomach felt packed full of sharp-edged rocks.

"Sit at the table," she ordered.

I sat down at her kitchen table.

"Don't scrape the chair on the floor. Pick it up when you move it," she growled at me.

"I'm sorry." I tried to not do anything else wrong.

She scooped from a pot on her stove and placed a bowl of soup and a couple of thick slices of bread in front of me. She didn't offer me any butter, and I was afraid to ask.

The soup tasted really good. It had chunks of meat in it, along with pieces of potato, carrot, and celery. The bread was homemade, and it tasted better than the thin slices of Wonder Bread we ate at home. I had a difficult time enjoying the food because my stomach was so tight from worrying what was going to happen next.

I hoped Naomi really wasn't as mean as she acted and looked. "Where are the dogs?" I asked.

"Don't talk with food in your mouth," she barked. "The dogs are in the backyard."

"Can I visit them when I'm done eating?" I asked.

"No."

"Why can't I?"

"Because I said you can't!" she gave me a vicious stare. "Don't argue with me."

I wasn't sure how dangerous Naomi really was, so I kept quiet and finished my dinner. After having teachers slap my face at school, I was careful not to irritate adults. If a kid was on their feet and had plenty of room to dodge and run, it was safer. Sitting down with grown-ups towering over and crowding you wasn't a smart time to push your luck. I couldn't wait to get away from this beastly woman.

After I'd eaten every bit of the food, she'd given me, I carried my dishes over to the sink.

"Follow me," she said.

Naomi led me through her apartment and out to the alcove. The pretty stained-glass window in the top half of the front door made the area light and friendly. She pointed to the stairway that went to the second floor.

"Go ahead of me," she ordered.

We climbed the thickly carpeted steps. I hated having Naomi close behind me. She could easily hit me on the back of my head the way my two older brothers did. When I was a toddler, as soon as I learned to walk, I learned to be aware of where my brothers were. Of course, if big Naomi walked ahead of me and fell backwards, she'd crush me as flat as a pancake.

We reached the second-floor landing, and she unlocked the door just to the right of the top floor apartment's entry door. "This will be your room." She gasped for breath after the climb up the stairway. She motioned me into the room. "If you have to use the bathroom, come downstairs and ring my doorbell."

"Can I go out and play?"

"No."

"It's still light out."

"Are you hard of hearing, boy?" She started to raise her hand as if to hit me but reconsidered. "I said no. I've already told you not to argue with me. And be quiet, so you don't bother the people who rent the apartment."

She turned away. Her wide back disappeared as she slammed the door behind her.

I checked out the room. Its only window overlooked Hamlin Avenue. The street was busy with traffic and a couple of kids walked along the sidewalk. I thought of Tommy and Ben and wondered what they were doing this very moment. I knew I'd be back with them tomorrow. As soon as I told Mom how much I disliked Naomi, my life would be back to normal. Everything would be okay.

The room Naomi left me in was crowded with a double-size bed, a dresser, and a nightstand. I pulled out the single drawer of the nightstand. There were two books in it. The Bible I knew. The other book, Pilgrim's Progress, was new to me. I picked it up and flipped through the pages. I didn't understand all the words and I was confused by the way they were put together. Without any pictures at all, it looked really boring. Lately, the only books I liked to read were comic books.

I opened the door to the closet. It contained rolls of fabric, stacks of crinkly-paper patterns, colorful round tins of buttons and lots of other sewing supplies. There wasn't anything I was interested in. I closed the door and looked out the window again. It was growing dark outside, and streetlamps, car headlights and house lights began to appear. People arriving home from work walked along the sidewalks. A city bus lumbered noisily along the street.

I turned on the single bare bulb overhead. It glowed harshly, but I was used to that. We always had bare-bulb overhead lights in the slums. I hadn't seen or heard any rats yet, and I appreciated that. I still listened closely for the awful scratchy sounds of claws and the thumping of bodies against the inside of the plaster walls, and ceiling above, or behind the furniture.

I sat on the edge of the bed. I couldn't stay still. My legs swung, my feet banged against the bed frame, and I twitched with nervous energy. I went to the window and looked out again. An older woman struggled along the sidewalk pulling a handcart of groceries behind her. She was probably on her way home to cook a delicious meal for her family. I wanted so much to be back with Mom and my brothers. I hated being alone in this room. I turned away from the window and sat on the bed again. I struggled not to cry. I really wanted to go downstairs and ask Naomi if she'd change her mind and let me go outside to play.

Would she?

Wouldn't she?

I doubted she'd say yes. Anyway, I was afraid of her and didn't want to be near her or talk to her. Oh hell. I was trapped in this room. But tomorrow, I'd be free again. I could wait until then. I undressed, turned off the light and crawled under the covers. The sheets were thick, clean and cool to my skin. The two blankets smelled fresh. I pulled the covers completely over my head and thought about Mom and Ben and Tommy. The damn tears started. I curled up into a tight ball. I still had hope. There was no way Mom would leave me here. I knew that for sure. She'd come tomorrow to reclaim me. She'd tell me how much she'd missed me. She'd promise to never leave me behind again. Now, I was sobbing like a damn baby. The crying convulsions went all the way through my body to the tip of my toes. My stomach tightened into a knot and snot dripped from my nose.

Sleep came to me. So, did a nightmare.

Naomi pushed Mom out the front door of her fancy house. I struggled to get past the big brute, but she held me back with her fat arm. Mom reached out for me. *"Mickey! Mickey, my pretty baby! I'm so sorry. You don't have to stay here. I love you, Mickey. You're coming home with me."*

I pushed the covers off my head. I kicked as hard as I could, trying to free my feet. I almost woke up, but I couldn't stay awake. I couldn't escape my horrible dream.

Mom and Tommy and Ben skipped down a sidewalk. They were laughing, and they called out to me. "Come on Mickey. Catch up to us." I tried my best to run after them, but I fell flat onto the ground and couldn't get up. Naomi stood over me. She cackled like the meanest witch from a scary movie. She rose up into the air just above me, and her breath was a spray of stinking fire that enveloped and burned me to a crisp.

I kicked myself free from the heavy blankets. I was burning up. I forced my eyes to open. I was still in a strange and scary room. I was still alone. I pulled the covers back over my head.

I relived the day Mom left me with Rose and George. I watched my mother walk away and leave me behind. I screamed deep inside of myself as she had walked away and left me alone with strangers. Not one person from my family was around me anymore. I'd been abandoned and forgotten by everyone I ever knew.

But, after a year, Mom did come back and reclaim me. She promised she wouldn't ever abandon me again. She promised we'd be together forever.

Mom *had* to rescue me tomorrow, or I'd shrivel up like a worm on a hot sidewalk and die.

In the total blackness under the covers, I sweated and struggled to breathe. Finally, I pushed the covers off my head. I was in semi-darkness with scary shadows shifting across the ceiling and walls. I remembered I was still in the room of a stranger's house. I was afraid to call out for help. I didn't want anyone to hear me except Mom. I didn't want anyone else to know how frightened I was. I screamed silently. "AAAAAAAH." Again, and again, I screamed silently until my throat was raw. Exhausted, I pulled the covers back over my head. I fell asleep. This time, I found an escape in sleep without nightmares.

Chapter 5

Daylight streaming through the window woke me. I lay in the strange bed. I couldn't remember where I was. Slowly, it came back to me. My mother left me with a stranger yesterday. But she was coming back today to rescue me. I climbed out of bed and dressed. I walked down the stairway to the first floor. I entered the vestibule and pushed the button outside Naomi's door. I heard the muted chime of the bell. After a few seconds, heavy footsteps approached. The door opened roughly. There stood the heavy body and the big head with its mean, ugly face. It wasn't just a nightmare. Naomi was real.

"Come in," She ordered as she struggled for breath.

She turned her broad back to me, and I followed her into her apartment.

"Shut the door behind you!"

I pushed the door shut.

"Don't slam the door!"

"I'm sorry."

I sat at the kitchen table while Naomi cooked breakfast for me. She set a couple of fried eggs and buttered toast in front of me. I loved fried eggs, which we rarely had at home. As I ate, I watched her work. I couldn't think of anything to say to her. She didn't act interested in talking to me anyway. The eggs and toast were delicious. I wanted to ask for more, but she seemed to be in a rotten mood, so I resisted. Even though she scared me, it wouldn't be so horrible living here if I got to eat fried eggs every morning.

"I ate everything, ma'am. Thanks for breakfast."

"Bring your dishes over here to the sink."

I did as I was told. I stood next to her because I didn't know what I was supposed to do.

"You're standing in my way." She used her elbow to shove me aside.

Naomi turned to look me in the eye. Her face was hard and mean. In a harsh voice, she said, "There's something you need to understand, Mickey." The tone of her voice and the way she said my name terrified me. "Your mother is going to leave you here, no matter what. She's already decided that." I didn't believe what she was saying, and I wanted to argue, but her size intimidated me. "Don't complain to your mother and create trouble for yourself. She doesn't want you anymore. She wants rid of you. Do you understand?"

"I guess," I mumbled.

There was no way Mom would leave me with this nasty woman. Naomi was a terrible liar. Mom loved me. Naomi was cruel and wanted to scare me. How could she know what my mother would do when they'd only talked for half an hour?

"You might as well go out to the yard and see the dogs."

I was so glad to get away from her. The food had been delicious, but she smelled like a dead skunk, and I didn't want to be close to her.

From the kitchen, I found my way through the screened, back porch sunroom and down some wooden steps. Both her dogs approached me. One was friendly, the other growled. I petted the friendly one. He wagged his tail and slobbered all over my hand. The unfriendly dog stayed a few feet away and gave me a fierce, warning look. Dogs didn't trust boys my age, but I was sure I could win him over.

The sun was warming up the day. Naomi's backyard didn't look too bad, a small patch of green lawn, a small garden plot and a garage that opened to the alley. There was probably some interesting stuff in the garage.

I was too anxious to enjoy the dogs or the outside much. I sat on the back-porch steps waiting for Mom's return. Both dogs got bored. They circled, lay down in upright positions and stared at me. Soon, they lost all interest and rolled on their sides, closed their eyes and snoozed.

I sat on the steps in a daze. I was glad to be away from Naomi, but I longed to be back with my mother and brothers. A bumblebee buzzed me. I ducked away from the damn thing. I zigzagged around the backyard to escape the scary insect that kept trying to land on my face. Damn bees. The unfriendly dog followed me. He stayed a few feet distant but glared at me. I think he wanted to snarl but controlled himself. His glare was enough to scare most people.

I walked along the narrow walkway that led to the alley and looked through the garage's side-door window. It was too gloomy-dark to see much except the bulk of a car and lots of spider webs. Deadly black widows, I imagine. There might be rats with their nasty little babies nesting in one of the dark, spider-webbed corners. I strolled back to the house and sat on the rear porch steps. I wanted to take a long nap, but even more, I wanted to cry, but I didn't want Naomi to see me being a crybaby. I didn't want the dogs to see me as a crybaby either.

The time crawled by so slow it hurt. I dozed off and on, but I couldn't get into a comfortable enough position to sleep on the wooden stairs.

The damn bumblebee buzzed me again. I jumped up and dodged away from it. I hated all insects, especially those that could fly. I laid down in a shady spot on the grass and quickly fell asleep.

"Your mother's here," Naomi shouted from her back door.

Mom! She'd come back for me. I jumped up and dodged around the two dogs and ran up the stairs. I stumbled and fell banging my knee. Ouch! Damn. I quickly recovered and ran into the house. There she stood.

"Mom! I was waiting for you!"

"Mickey!" Mom showed her wonderful smile. I ran into her arms. She gave me a loving hug and kiss. This time, I hugged her back with all my strength. I was so overjoyed to see her, I barely noticed the pain in my knee.

Chapter 6

I felt dizzy with relief as Mom and I rode away in a taxi and left Naomi behind us. I was glad I wouldn't ever be near the ugly cow again.

Soon, we were downtown among towering granite and brick buildings, lots of noisy traffic and thousands of people crowding the sidewalks.

"Please drop us off in front of Marshall Field, driver," Mom instructed the cabbie between puffs on her cigarette.

"Sure thing, lady," He winked at her through the rearview mirror. Damn hack.

We got out of the cab in front of the huge Marshall Field department store. Weaving our way through the mass of pedestrians, we entered through the thick glass and golden metal revolving door. I resisted the urge to speed the door up and bump people's heels the way Tommy and Ben liked to do. Now that Mom and I were back together, I'd behave for as long as I could. I followed closely behind her as we made our way past the fabulous items in this famous store. Oh, man. How wonderful it'd be to be rich and buy lots of expensive stuff!

We stopped in the boy's clothing area.

"We're going to buy new clothes for you, Mickey," Mom flashed me a big smile.

I couldn't remember ever having brand-new clothes. I always wore hand-me-downs from my older brothers.

She and I carefully picked out a pair of socks, one pair of undershorts, one undershirt, one pair of corduroy pants, a belt and a short-sleeve, button-up shirt. The new shoes she picked weren't Buster Browns, but they were similar, and I liked them anyway. Dazzled by the brightness and luxury of this store, I wondered why Mom was buying me new clothes, but there was no way I'd question her and make her think about how much money she was spending.

I went into the changing room and happily put on my new duds. When I walked out onto the main floor, Mom's face lit up with pride.

"You look very handsome, Mickey." She gave me a hug and a kiss, and the pretty saleslady said, "He certainly is handsome."

"Can you throw his old clothes away?" Mom asked.

"Sure, honey." The saleslady accepted my wadded-up bundle of worn and ripped clothes and tossed them into her trash receptacle.

I loved my brand-new wardrobe, but I worried what Tommy and Ben would do to me when we got home. Mom spent all that money on me in this famous store, and she didn't buy anything for them. They'll be horribly jealous, and I'll be in for some hard punches and painful scalp burns. So, what! Right now, I was in heaven.

We walked the three blocks to the downtown restaurant where Mom worked. Inside, it was bright, busy and noisy. Pans clanged in the kitchen, waitresses called out orders, dishes clattered, people talked loud, cigarette smoke filled the air, and I was so grateful to be with Mom and away from that beast, Naomi.

Since it was Mom's day off, she wore a dark blue skirt and a matching jacket with a white blouse. I thought she was more gorgeous than I'd ever seen her. I was proud to be with her, dressed in my new clothes. A man who appeared to be her boss led us to a booth. He was all smiles for us. He patted me on my shoulder and acted as if he actually liked kids. He certainly liked Mom. She always looked glamorous when she walked in her high-heeled shoes, and all the men in the restaurant turned and looked at her.

We had a booth to ourselves. I sat across from her with my elbows on the table and watched her light a cigarette. I remembered what Naomi had said about Mom leaving me no matter what. Jesus, those words scared the hell out of me! But I was sure such a terrible thing wasn't going to happen to me. Mom was being full of love, and I knew she wouldn't ever leave me with strangers again.

Lots of the waitresses stopped by our booth to say hello. Everybody in the world liked Mom.

A tall, smiling waitress took our order.

"Ginny, what a handsome boy he is. Such beautiful blonde hair and bright blue eyes. And that sweet baby face."

She winked at me as she turned away and headed for the kitchen. I didn't like the baby face part, but I did like how friendly she was.

All the waitresses wore the same neat uniform. Red and white checkered, with puffy sleeves and cut low enough in the front to show the top of their boobs and hemmed just below the knee to show off some leg.

Mom took a deep drag off her cigarette. She exhaled the smoke across the table and above my head. The smoke floated down and enveloped me. I coughed and my eyes watered, but Mom didn't notice. I was used to that. It was a small price to pay for being with her. I was sure I'd soon learn to smoke cigarettes as expertly as she did, and I'd blow out fancy streams of smoke.

Suddenly, Mom looked right at me, and she blurted out, "Mickey, I think it's a good idea for you to live with Naomi for a while."

My heart fell down into my stomach. I couldn't believe she'd said those horrible words. I felt like I'd piss my new pants. "What, Mom? I don't want to live there, Mom. I don't like that woman."

She looked off to the side to avoid my frantic look. "You have to stay there awhile, Mickey. Naomi is a good, Christian woman."

She hadn't recognized what a nasty, old cow Naomi was. Was she just pretending to be blind? What was going on with her? "Please, Mom.

She doesn't like me. I don't want to live with her."

She flicked cigarette ash into the ashtray. "She has a nice house. You'll have your own room and plenty of food. I can't take proper care of you right now."

"You said I wouldn't have to stay there if I didn't like it. You promised!"

She didn't answer me. A man walking by slowed down to smile at her and say hello. She smiled back at him. He ignored me completely.

The friendly waitress brought our food. Mine was a delicious looking cheeseburger with tomato and onions and mayonnaise, a side of potato chips and a large glass of Coca-Cola.

"Here you are, honey." The waitress winked at me as she set my beautiful lunch in front of me. I couldn't force any words out.

"Thanks," Mom said. "Remember your manners, Mickey."

I tried to force out a "Thank You," but I couldn't find my voice.

"You're welcome, Ginny," the waitress said to Mom. She turned to me with another big smile. "Enjoy your lunch, sweetie."

This waitress was almost as pretty as Mom. I might marry someone like her when I grow up. I was beginning to accept that I couldn't marry Mom. Never!

"Thanks," I yelled to the waitress as she walked away. She didn't turn to look back, but she did give me a little wave of her hand.

I looked at my lunch.

"As soon as my money situation is better, Mickey, I'll come and bring you back home," Mom said. She took a bite from her club sandwich.

"I want to be with you now, Mom. I want to be with you and Tommy and Ben," I pleaded. The damn tears started forcing their way out of my eyes. She wasn't listening to me. She wouldn't look me in the eye.

"You know Tommy ran away," she said. She took a drink of her coffee.

I took a bite of my cheeseburger, but it tasted like I'd stuffed a clump of dirt in my mouth.

"I'm still trying to find Tommy." She set her coffee down. Lipstick stained the rim of the brownish cup.

"Tommy will come back home, Mom," I said as I tried to chew my cardboard-tasting cheeseburger. "We can all be together, Mom. Our whole family can be together." I wiped away tears with the back of my hand. My nose dripped snot onto my new shirt and my lunch.

"It can't be that way right now, Mickey," she said. She drew away from me. I didn't know what I did that was so awful she wanted to be rid of me.

"I'm sure things will get better soon. Then, I'll bring you back home." She looked around the restaurant nervously and lit another cigarette. "Don't cry, Mickey. Be a big boy."

Suddenly, a ray of hope hit me. Mom was playing a terrible joke on me. I really wanted her to quit acting so mean. It wasn't like her to be this cruel.

"Be brave, Mickey," she said. "I had to quit school and go to work in a glove factory when I was only fourteen-years-old."

"I'm only nine-years-old, Mom."

"I loved school, and I had to quit," she said sadly. "I didn't have money to buy my own lunch when I was at work, and a woman offered me part of hers. I was so ashamed."

She looked terribly unhappy about being poor and having to quit school. Why was I such a whiner? I couldn't control myself. "I'll quit school and go to work, Mom. I'll help you out. Then, we can stay together."

"You can't quit school, Mickey. You're too young to go to work."

"I can shine shoes, Mom."

"No!"

"I can sell newspapers."

She took a really deep drag off her cigarette and looked at me like everything wrong with her life was my fault.

"You promised," I squeaked out while I tried to chew another bite of my cardboard cheeseburger.

There was a loud crash of dishes from the kitchen, and both of us flinched.

I finally swallowed the rest of the bite. It was one of the greatest lunches I'd ever had, but I couldn't enjoy it. I was hungry, but I couldn't eat.

"Please, Mom. I'll be good."

"That's not it, Mickey."

She stubbed her cigarette into the ashtray. Her face showed impatience. I could see she was tired of arguing with me. It was at least the fourth cigarette she'd smoked during lunch. She took money out of her purse and laid it on the table. She'd eaten only a couple of bites of her sandwich.

"Let's go, Mickey."

Frantic with fear, I was barely able to stand up. As I followed her, I couldn't feel my legs or my feet. The waitresses waved goodbye as we went out the door. How could they be so cheerful? We left the restaurant and most of our lunch behind.

This ride in a cab with my mother was the scariest of them all. I sat as far away from her as I could. I didn't want her to be my mother anymore.

Cab and traffic sounds filled the silence. Metal squeaked, gears shifted, brakes squealed, and horns blew. She smoked cigarette after cigarette. Some of the smoke was sucked out through the partially opened windows. Some formed a cloud around my head. Mom didn't speak at all as we rode back to Naomi's. I hated it when she wouldn't talk to me. Why was she doing this? The cab driver looked back at us through the rearview mirror. He glanced at Mom and smiled stupidly. Why did men always have to flirt with her?

We pulled up in front of Naomi's house and parked.

"Please wait," Mom said to the cabbie. "I'll only be a moment."

As she and I exited the cab and walked up to Naomi's, I couldn't lift my feet or move them forward. There was still a chance Mom would change her mind and wouldn't do this terrible thing to me. As we climbed the concrete steps to the front porch, I struggled to maintain my balance. Naomi had seen us through her front window and rushed to fling the front door open. My hope that she was a terrible dream crumbled again. I felt an overwhelming urge to turn and run down the street as fast as I could force my legs to move. I wanted to run away from everyone in the world, including Mom, but I couldn't make my body do anything I wanted it to.

"Mickey has decided he wants to stay with you," Mom lied. "Here's twenty dollars for the first two weeks. I'll mail more after my next payday."

Naomi looked at the bills like they were counterfeit. She twisted and pulled at them to be sure they were real.

"Well," Naomi said. "Make sure you do send the money."

A sour taste came up from my stomach and settled in my throat and mouth. I wanted to puke all my insides out.

"I'll call soon to see how Mickey is doing."

Mom leaned over and gave me a quick hug and kiss. I couldn't feel the least bit of love in her touch. Why was this happening to me?

"Be a good boy, Mickey," she said. "I love you."

She turned and walked back to the cab. I listened to her footsteps, but I couldn't turn around and watch her leave. This was worse than the scariest nightmare I ever tried to wake up from. I heard the cab door shut. I listened to the cab pull away from the curb. I didn't want to look, but I had to see if she'd really left me. The cab with Mom inside it disappeared down the avenue. It felt like a huge machine was mangling my insides. It was the worst pain I ever felt.

"Come inside," Naomi ordered.

I stepped through the doorway of her house. The door slammed shut behind me.

Chapter 7

Naomi, Emil, the boarder and I shared an immaculately clean bathroom in their apartment on the first floor. A ceramic sculpture of Jesus Christ the Savior hung on the wall above the toilet. Jesus wore a flowing robe; his hands were outstretched with his palms showing and a halo glowed around his head. The words just below his nail-pierced feet read, "Jesus Loves You." I wasn't sure Jesus loved me anymore. Above the bathroom's pedestal sink hung a mirror. As I washed my hands, I stared at my reflection. What I saw didn't disgust me. I looked more closely at myself in the mirror. I couldn't see why Mom didn't want me anymore. On this, my first day with Naomi, and the first time I used the toilet, I carelessly looked around while I stood and pissed.

Immediately afterwards, I stood in front of the scary woman in her living room. I waited to be told what to do. She walked quickly to the bathroom. After a few seconds, she burst out of there and rushed at me like one of the crazed stampeding elephants I'd seen in the movies. She grabbed me by my hair and twisted without mercy. Her grip on my hair made it impossible to break free. She dragged me towards the bathroom. My scalp separated from my skull. Searing pain where each strand of hair grew out of my scalp made me yelp like an injured puppy. No one ever pulled my hair so ruthlessly. Tears welled up in my eyes. I reached up and grabbed Naomi's hand. Her fingers were thick and strong. I felt each wrinkle and the creases of her knuckles. She wore a large ring that cut into my palm. She dug her fingernails into me. I pulled my wounded hands away. She picked up a heavy-heeled shoe from the floor.

She hit me on my head, my shoulders and my back with the hard, sharp heel of the shoe. She threw me to the floor.

"Don't you ever attack me, you filthy, little monster!" she screamed.

I curled into a ball as she kicked me several times on my back.

"Don't you ever fight back, you rotten slum boy!"

Fire-hot pain shot along my spine. I lay on the floor motionless, hoping she'd stop kicking me.

"Get into the bathroom you pig. Clean up the mess you made. Don't ever do a filthy thing like that again!"

I didn't understand what she was screaming about until I saw the dribbles of urine on the rim of the toilet seat and the floor.

As I cleaned up my mess with my shirt sleeve, my nerves vibrated. I hoped she didn't attack me as soon as I walked out of the bathroom.

While she cooked her husband's dinner, I sat at the kitchen table avoiding her angry eyes as she screeched warnings to me in her raspy voice. I flinched whenever she came close to me.

"You do what I tell you to do when I tell you. Don't raise your hand to me. Don't touch me. You belong in an orphanage or reform school. If you don't behave, I'll call the police and have them throw you in jail, and you'll spend the rest of your life there. I don't know why I'm giving you a home. Nobody else would let a thing like you live in their house."

I cringed under the fury of her loud, verbal assault.

"Emil, my husband, is an important tool and die-maker. Don't bother him. Don't talk to him. When he comes home, he scrubs his hands at the kitchen sink. Don't get in his way. Leave him alone. Do you understand?"

"Yes, ma-am," I squeaked.

I heard the front door open. It must be her husband. I was terrified. He might be even bigger and meaner than she was. Maybe he'd hit me harder than she did.

But his footsteps weren't heavy. He entered the kitchen.

"This is the boy I told you about." Her voice dripped with disapproval and disappointment.

I looked up at him. He nodded at me.

He wasn't a huge monster like her. He didn't look dangerous and mean. He didn't show much interest in me at all. I felt a tiny bit of relief.

Emil spoke with a Swedish accent. Thinning grey hair framed his pale, unsmiling face. He was a bit shorter than Naomi, but much thinner and wore dark-blue workman's clothes. He reminded me of the tiny mouse next to a huge elephant in the movie cartoons. Naomi and Emil didn't hug each other. They barely talked to each other. She served him a delicious dinner of roast beef, boiled potatoes and brown gravy in their dining room.

I sat by myself in the kitchen eating stew and slices of plain bread. The pieces of meat in the stew were small but delicious. I wanted more than she gave me but was afraid to ask. She got angry quick and hit hard.

"It's time to go up to your room and to bed," she ordered.

It was still light out, but I was too frightened of her temper to argue.

"Here is an alarm clock. Pull the alarm-switch out every night. The alarm will go off at five A.M. I want you down here immediately. Don't make me climb those stairs to wake you up.".

I trudged up the carpeted stairway to my new room. I wasn't used to such quiet. I missed being bumped and teased by my two older brothers. God, I wish they were here with me now. Tommy would've hit Naomi dead center in her face with his baseball bat. Smack. Crash. She'd fall to the floor as dead as a cow at the slaughterhouse. My last school took us on a tour of the slaughterhouse and the bloody killing floor where they used a sledgehammer to knock the animals out before they gutted them with a knife. I hadn't imagined they killed cows and horses that way. At this moment, I'd like to see Naomi die that way.

When I opened the door to my room, bright daylight streamed

through the window, but I couldn't bear to look out onto the street. I didn't want to think about how far I was from home and Mom and my brothers. I undressed and crawled into bed. Everything would be different after a night's sleep. I curled up into a ball and pulled the covers over my head. I needed to hide from my horrible new life. I prayed Mom would change her mind and rush back to rescue me. She'd wrap her arms around me. With tears streaming down her face, she'd tell me how sorry she was for being so cruel. If she didn't come back tomorrow, she'd surely come the day after tomorrow. I couldn't possibly live with Naomi longer than that.

In the dark, under the covers, I cried until my eyes hurt. My nose dripped a ton of snot, and my stomach ached. I didn't remember falling asleep.

I was running. A skid-row drunk my brothers and I robbed was chasing us. The slobbering demon got closer and closer to me. Off in the distance, Tommy and Ben yelled "Catch up, Mickey! Run faster." I couldn't run faster. I couldn't catch up to my brothers. I couldn't even see them anymore. The foul-smelling drunk reached out his long-nailed, scabby-fingered hand and grabbed me by the hair, pulled me backwards and threw me to the ground. As he cursed me his spit landed on my face. With his sharp-pointed boots, he kicked me with all his strength. I struggled to wake up. I wanted to escape the nightmare and the pain. My eyelids felt glued shut.

Again, a pain in my side. Again, a harsh voice. I pushed away from the demon's vicious assault and forced my eyes open. I focused on the face and the bright ceiling light above me. It wasn't the enraged drunk. It was that woman. It was that terrible woman Mom had left me with. I struggled to remember her name.

"Wake up!" She poked me again with her sharp-pointed fingernail. "Why didn't you get up?"

"I'm sorry. I didn't know how to work the clock."

"You're really stupid, aren't you?"

"I'm sorry. I didn't know how."

"Shut up and get dressed. Come downstairs immediately. This better never happen again, or you'll be sorry."

She stormed out of the room and slammed the door shut behind her. I hurried to do what I was told.

Mom didn't rush back to rescue me. Not the next day nor the next day nor the next. I couldn't believe that living with Naomi was really my new life. She was too frightening. Please, God. Don't let it be.

On the terrible day my mother had left me with Naomi, I wore the wonderful new clothes Mom had bought for me when we shopped at the Marshall Field store downtown.

"Change into these," Naomi ordered. She handed me a pile of odd-looking garments. "Fold up those new clothes your mother bought you and give them to me."

I went into the bathroom and took off the best clothes I ever owned. The new outfit Naomi gave me was many sizes too large. I pulled on the big man trousers. I put on the faded-yellow, checked, man's shirt. I needed to roll up the pant legs and shirtsleeves many times to find my feet and hands. I pulled onto my feet a pair of floppy mismatched socks and a pair of worn, high-top leather shoes several sizes too large for my feet.

I stared at myself in the bathroom mirror. My skinny body was no more than a few sticks holding up a ridiculous, scarecrow costume.

"Why can't I wear the new clothes my Mom bought for me?" I whined when I stood in front of Naomi again.

Her hand moved very fast. She slapped me full on my cheek. I saw a blazing flash of lights as I fell to the floor. My face throbbed with pain.

"Don't argue with me!" she screamed.

I curled my body into a tight ball with my arms next to my face. I feared she'd now kick me. I hated the taste of my own warm blood filling my mouth. I was afraid to spit it out onto her floor and swallowed it instead.

Chapter 8

The house Naomi and Emil Johnson owned was a flat-roofed, two-story brick structure with a full basement. The basement's half-windows showed just above ground level. Naomi and Emil lived in the first-floor apartment. They rented a first-floor bedroom to a single male, and a second-floor apartment to a couple in their late forties. When I reached the landing, the door on the right was for my room. Immediately to the left was the door to the rented apartment. A door in my room led to their front room, but it was locked, with furniture set against it on their side. I clearly heard their conversations and television through that barricaded door.

The harsh ring of the alarm clock startled me from a deep sleep. I reluctantly crawled out of my warm bed while it was still dark outside

My first destination was the basement to clean out the furnace and add new coal. Naomi was angry she had to climb down the narrow, wooden staircase to supervise me during my learning period. Terrified of her anger, I struggled to complete the work to her satisfaction. She kept clenching her fists as she instructed me. I trembled, and my mind whirled as I tried to remember every one of her harsh commands. I constantly feared making a mistake and her attacking me with her fists again.

I opened the furnace door and worked as fast as I could to break up the clinkers of burned-up coal with a long, metal poker. I cleaned out the ashes and threw any usable coal back in the furnace. A couple of burns on my hands and arms from bumping into the red-hot metal surfaces taught me to be careful.

I scooped big chunks of coal from the nearby coal room with a wide-mouth shovel and carried them to the furnace. The shovel was heavy, and with a full load I could barely balance and carry the weight. When that shovel twisted sideways and dumped the coal on the floor, I worked faster to recover the lost time.

I wasn't strong or skilled enough to do my jobs speedily and perfectly, but that didn't earn any sympathy from Naomi.

After I finished the furnace work, I washed the morning dishes. Then, on my hands and knees, I scrubbed and waxed the linoleum and wood floors throughout her apartment.

Naomi baked and roasted lots of delicious food for her and Emil to eat. Every few days, I cleaned the kitchen oven with a noxious gunk that bubbled and smoked and made my nostrils ache.

Several days a week, I scrubbed linens and other laundry on a washboard in a pair of side-by-side tubs in the basement. I rubbed my knuckles raw and bloody against the ribbed-metal surface. Naomi's homemade lye-soap made the open cuts and scrapes on my hands sting like hell. After I scrubbed each article clean on the board, I lifted it into the second tub of clean rinse water and doused them until I got all the soap out. I had to change the rinse water frequently. The tough job was wringing the water out of the thick and heavy items by hand.

In summer, I hung the laundry outside on the clothesline. Sometimes, a soft breeze of warm, clean air ruffled the laundry, but often the air was laden with coal soot from the city's many furnaces. Dirty flecks settled on the laundry I'd worked so hard to get clean. Naomi yelled at me as if the soot was my fault and made me rewash that laundry.

In winter, I hung the wash in the basement where coal bin dust and furnace smoke mocked my efforts to end up with white linens.

I didn't have big hands or much muscle, so it took all my strength to wring the water out of the bed sheets and towels. If I left too much water in the clothes, they were heavier to carry and took longer to dry, especially on cold days. Frozen sheets on the backyard clotheslines made quite a sight, but Naomi didn't find it funny.

When I hung the laundry in the basement, it dripped on the concrete floor if I didn't wring every last drop of water out. If Naomi navigated her way down the stairway and saw puddles of water, she'd scream at me, grab me by my hair, slap my face and kick me. It took me a while to perfect this work, so I got used to being hit.

"Stupid!" she yelled at me again and again.

The monster liked to hit me with the broomstick she used as a walking cane. I tried to dodge her blows, but when I resisted too much, she chased me down and hit me more and harder.

For Emil's breakfast every day, Naomi served fried-eggs, bacon, fried potatoes, and buttered toast. He ate his meals at the dining room table. After I finished my morning work, I sat at the kitchen table and ate a bowl of lumpy, yellow cornmeal and a slice of dry toast. At seven-thirty, I left for school.

"I want you home directly after school," Naomi warned me, as we walked the seven blocks to my new school. She gasped for breath from the exertion. "If you're late, you'll be really sorry."

She had to go along the first day to register me at Ryerson Elementary School. I wore my raggedy, oversized old-man clothes.

"His name is Mickey Johnson," Naomi told the woman in the school office.

"My name is Mickey Shafer," I blurted out.

Naomi's big elbow hit me on the side of my head, directly on my ear. That really hurt.

"He's mixed up. He's not real smart. His name is Johnson," Naomi explained.

"Hello, Mickey Johnson." The woman behind the counter frowned down at me.

I didn't want to have a new last name, but there wasn't anything I could do about it. I stayed silent.

"His school records were lost," Naomi lied.

"All his records were lost?" the woman asked as she peered over the counter again and looked at me like I was a stray dog.

"That's right," Naomi said.

"Are those his school clothes?" The woman looked at me with great concern.

"Yes, they are." Naomi replied defiantly.

I stood next to Naomi in my raggedy clothes, with my head bowed. I was afraid to speak. I didn't want her elbow smashing into my ear again.

"Okay. We'll try him in the third grade and see how he does. There are several slow students in the class he'll be in."

Chapter 9

Ryerson School was a three-story, brick building with metal stairways between the floors. The footsteps of running and bouncing children resonated loudly. Thirty-eight desks and forty-one students crowded the classroom I was assigned to. I stood at the very back of the room waiting for the school to make reassignments and maybe then a desk would be available for me.

"If anyone raises their hand to ask a question before I'm ready, I'll cut their arm off and throw it out the window," the teacher announced loudly. She was younger, but she reminded me of Naomi: she sounded angry like her too.

She called roll.

"George Harris."

"Present."

"Carol Sanders."

"Present."

"Mickey Johnson."

I heard bodies shifting.

"Mickey Johnson!" she called louder.

I listened to the sound of throats clearing. I wished the stupid kid, Mickey Johnson, would answer this woman so she wouldn't call his name any louder. She got angrier each time he ignored her. I was surprised there was another Mickey in this school.

"Mickey Johnson!" The teacher yelled even louder. Her face had turned a glowing red.

She walked heavily down the aisle toward me.

I was terrified by the approach of her large body and the sound of her heavy footsteps. My throat was parched as dry as a desert, and my butthole tightened more than ever before. I was as frightened as when Tommy and Ben shut me in the dark stairway to our building's basement and held the door. Rats swarmed below me, and I waited for those vermin to climb up the steps to rip my bare feet apart.

She towered over me. "Mickey Johnson!"

She was as huge and as frightening as Naomi.

"Don't you know your own name?"

"Huh?"

"HUH!" She repeated with derision.

Laughter rose from my classmates.

"He's a retard," a voice near me said loudly.

"Shut up. All of you. Just shut up." The teacher looked around the room. Her fury-distorted face rotated slowly. She looked back down at me. "Mickey Johnson!" she thundered. She loomed over me, and I felt a terrible urge to piss.

"Present," I whispered out in my tiny, frightened voice. Please, Jesus, don't let me piss my pants.

"Well, you do know your name!" Her voice dripped with disdain. She turned and marched back up the aisle to the front of the classroom. The floor vibrated under her.

I wanted to explain. There was a good reason I didn't know my own name. I didn't remember Naomi gave me a new name. I hadn't had time to absorb such a drastic change. But it was too late. I listened as the whispers continued. "He's a retard."

"He's an idiot."

"He's a moron."

"He's really stupid."

Chain-link fenced the Ryerson School playground. Stubborn weeds worked their way through the numerous cracks in sun-tortured, black asphalt. Weathered, wooden backboards mounted on rusty poles with nets of tattered chain-link equipped the basketball courts. For the weak and frightened children, this was a war-zone dominated by cruel, strutting bullies. Before and after school and during recess, the playground was a true hell even the Lord Jesus Christ wouldn't venture onto.

I did my best to adjust to the terrible clothes Naomi forced me to wear. Every step was a challenge to keep my oversized shoes on and stay upright. In a fistfight, I swung at my tormentors, but couldn't connect. My feet refused to obey me, and I careened about like a drunk as the bullies easily dodged and laughed at me.

I resembled the famous tramp in the movies, except I couldn't dance, and I didn't have a cane to help me fight off my enemies. My clothes were far uglier than the clothes the funny tramp bounced around in.

I was comical.

I was an object of ridicule.

"What a retard."

"Don't you know how to walk, spastic?"

"You look like a total freak in those weird clothes."

I was fun to pick a fight with.

"Come on, dummy. I'm going to kick your ass."

I didn't have my two older brothers, Tommy and Ben, to help me.

I entered the school stairwell to climb from floor to floor.

I needed to climb the stairs from the first to the third floor in my floppy shoes. I held onto the handrail as I struggled upward. I moved slowly and lifted my feet with uncertainty. Normal children scurried up and down those stairs at high speed. I often encountered a student or a teacher who wouldn't concede the handrail to me. I had to let go of my lifeline. I was bumped and jostled by people who were quicker and more sure-footed than I was. I leaned forward because it was okay to fall forward onto my knees, but I didn't want to be pitched backwards and crack the back of my head wide open.

Despite my best efforts, I was knocked backwards. I twisted awkwardly and fell down several stairs. I tried to stand but was pushed down several more steps. I gave up on standing and crawled upwards on my hands and my knees, desperate to reach the landing between the floors.

"Get up onto your feet, retard."

"Learn how to walk, dummy."

Reaching the landing was a great triumph!

A solid shove from an older student sent me sprawling. As I fell, my shoes shifted position on my feet. Dazed, I sat up and leaned against the wall. I saw that the toes of my shoes were pointing sideways. I reached forward and straightened them. I desperately needed to continue my climb and reach the third floor. People stepped on me, people bumped into me, and the meanest people kicked me.

"Get out of the way, you freak."

Finally, I reached the third floor. I was close.

I'd missed the tardy bell again. I clomped into the classroom. All the kids sat at their desks, and all eyes turned to watch me. Laughter rolled across the room.

"It's the circus clown," a childish voice proclaimed.

They were right. I'd make a great clown in the circus. I'd be perfect as one of those pitiful clowns that constantly stumbled, fell and injured themselves. Thousands of people would laugh at my misfortune and pain. My misery would entertain everyone.

I now had my own desk in the classroom. I'd learned to write my real name, Mickey Shafer, but since Naomi changed my last name to her last name, I had to remember to write the new name she'd forced on me. I kept forgetting my new last name was Johnson. I tried to avoid making more mistakes and provoking anger from the teacher and laughter from my merciless classmates. My repeated failures kept me in such constant panic I couldn't think clearly.

The teacher stood over me again. "Why are you writing Shafer? Your name is Johnson. You should be able to remember that."

"Yes, ma'am." I was trembling. I didn't want to answer her harsh interrogation. I didn't want to breathe.

"How old are you, Mickey?"

"I'm nine, ma'am."

"When is your birthday?"

"It's February sixth." I felt better about myself.

"You have to learn to spell F-e-b-r-u-a-r-y correctly." Her voice grew louder each time she scolded me.

"Yes, ma'am."

"Ha. Ha." The familiar laughter rolled across the classroom.

"You're such a retard."

"You dress like an old bum."

"You walk like a gimp."

"Shut up!" the teacher yelled.

I hung my head and stared at my desktop. The only place I could hide was deep inside of my own mind, and my mind wouldn't stop whirling.

Alone in my room at Naomi's house, nightmares of not being able to walk tortured me.

I teetered helplessly in huge clown shoes and wandered into a pit of quicksand. The bubbling muck grabbed my legs, and I sank up to my neck. Horror of suffocation swept over me. I struggled to rise up and escape the deadly quagmire, but I kept sinking until my head was completely covered and I couldn't breathe.

I woke up kicking. My feet were completely tangled in the blanket like I'd fallen flat while in a sack race, and my face was covered. Drenched in sweat and trembling with panic, I cried out, "Mom!" I finally freed myself from the entrapment. I could breathe again. I tossed the covers off, but quickly became chilled and reluctantly pulled the covers back up.

When I found sleep, I was back in the quicksand. A pair of strong hands grabbed my ankles and pulled me down into the morass. I struggled to free myself from the demon that had latched onto me, but my whole body sank deeper and deeper into the mire. I kicked as hard as I could. I reached up for rescue. I couldn't breathe. Save me, Jesus.

I woke up. I'd pushed my covers onto the floor. I took deep breaths and focused on the reflections of the nighttime auto traffic lights shifting across the walls and ceiling.

"Mom! Please come back and save me, Mom! Please. I'll never do anything bad again."

Chapter 10

Large, angry Naomi stood over me, her hands clenched into fists.

"Your mother only sent me ten dollars twice. She promised to pay me ten dollars every week for giving you a home. The manager of the restaurant where she waitressed said she didn't show up for work last week. He said she disappeared, and nobody knows where she went."

I held back my tears.

"I never believed your mother could be trusted. That bitch just wanted rid of you."

Spit flew from Naomi's mouth and landed on me.

"I'm sorry," I apologized.

"Sorry! I don't want to hear any 'I'm sorry' from you."

Her face reddened, and her breathing grew harsh.

"You're going to have to work harder. I didn't take you into my house out of charity. You're costing me money. Your mother promised me ten dollars a week for giving you a place to live."

"Will I be allowed to play outside?"

"No, you won't. How stupid can you be? You have to earn your room and your food. Would you like me to throw you out on the street with the rest of the orphans? Nobody else wants something like you. You're lucky I'm letting you stay here. I should get rid of you like your mother did."

"My mother will come back for me. She promised she would"

"Oh, you think so? You're so stupid."

Naomi stepped over to the fireplace. She took a piece of paper out of a fine, china container that sat on the fireplace mantle.

"Look at this, stupid" she spit out. "It's the advertisement from the newspaper. You want to hear what it says?"

I didn't reply. She fumbled as she unfolded the tiny bit of newsprint and squinted at the scrap of newspaper.

"Loving home wanted for a nine-year-old boy."

She looked up from the paper and glared at me with disgust. "He is well behaved. He is healthy. He has blond hair and blue eyes."

She said blond hair and blue eyes like they were something filthy.

"Mother will pay ten dollars a week."

I struggled to take all of this in. My brain wasn't working.

"Your own mother put this ad in the newspaper to get rid of you. Why would she come back for you?"

I didn't understand why Naomi was so angry with me. It was like she hated me.

"That ten dollars a week your mother promised me was a lie!"

Her face turned purple and mad-dog foam formed on her lower lip.

"Your mother said she'd pay me ten dollars a week!" she screamed, "Your mother is a filthy liar!"

I cringed under the force of her rage.

"My mother isn't a liar," I protested feebly.

"Don't talk back to me."

She stepped closer to me. She slapped at my face. Her fingernails caught my cheek. I put my hands up in front of my face to block her. She grabbed my hands. "I told you not to put your hands up like that!" Her face twisted into a devil mask.

She held both my hands with one of hers. Her fingernails dug into my skin. She used her free hand to slap my cheek. It really stung. My sight went blurry, and tears forced their way from my eyes.

"Your mother is a liar!" She swung again and hit me full on my ear. My ear went numb, but my brain throbbed with pain.

There was nothing I could say. The truth crushed me. After she quit hitting me and she released my hands, I went back to scrubbing her floor. I kept my head bowed low, afraid to look up at her. I didn't want to be hit anymore. She told me I had to hold my face up and leave it unprotected. I couldn't do that. I couldn't stop my hands from trying to deflect her fists.

"Your mother is a liar and a whore," she screeched.

I wanted to kill her for saying that about Mom.

George and Rose had wanted to keep me. They'd been terribly upset and visibly angry when I wanted to go home with my mother. George and Rose had talked about adopting me. I still wasn't sure what adoption really meant, except they'd have owned me forever. It didn't matter now. I'd made an awful decision.

When George and Rose took me into their home, I was seven-years-old. Even though they'd worried I was too old of a kid to take a chance with, they gave me a home. I'd just squeezed under the desirable-age-bar because I looked younger than my seven years. I appeared innocent and soft. George and Rose had no idea of the terrible things I'd done on the streets of Chicago with my two older brothers.

There wouldn't ever be another chance of a loving home for somebody like me. Nobody would adopt a wicked nine-year-old boy.

Chapter 11

As I scrubbed Naomi's wood floors on my hands and knees with a bucket of soapy water and a rag, I maneuvered around her bulky furniture. I spilled a tiny bit of water on one of her area rugs as I moved the bucket.

"Be careful, you fool!" Naomi yelled. She kicked me in my side. I gasped for breath as a surge of pain traveled through my body. My ribs throbbed from the impact of her hard-toed shoe. I was sure if she kept kicking me, she'd break every bone in my body.

My high-top, leather shoes thudded against one of Naomi's end tables.

"Don't be so clumsy, you idiot!" she screamed. She hit me across my back with the broomstick she used as a cane. The skin on my back felt on fire. I feared if she kept hitting me with her broomstick, I'd collect hundreds of scars on my back. I'd look just like the chain gang convicts in the movies. After years of imprisonment and whippings, their beaten backs were a maze of crisscrossed scars.

I bumped into a small round table with my elbow. One of the monster's silver-framed pictures fell over.

"Watch what you're doing, stupid!" She kicked me violently on my thigh. My leg muscles cramped and produced a terrible pain. I feared my leg would die and rot away and have to be sawed from my body. I'd become a one-legged, street bum on Chicago's skid row streets.

"If you break the glass on one of my pictures, you're going to be really sorry, you clumsy oaf."

I wasn't as tough as I needed to be. Like a whiny sissy, I wished I had my older brothers, Tommy and Ben, at my side to help me in my battle against this female Frankenstein.

I didn't know how to fight a woman, especially a woman as large and cruel as Naomi. She weighed at least two-hundred-pounds while I weighed fifty pounds at the most. She was much stronger than me. If I had a baseball bat like my oldest brother, Tommy, carried when we rolled drunks on Chicago's skid row, I could smash her on her head, and her skull would split apart like a dropped watermelon. Then, I'd be free. But I didn't have a baseball bat. And, I didn't want to go to prison and be locked in a dark, rat-infested dungeon. I didn't want to be beaten with thick, wooden clubs and rubber hoses by gloating prison guards. I didn't want to be fried to a crisp in the electric chair screaming in agony with my eyeballs bulging out from my head.

I repressed thoughts of physical resistance to the monster, but they didn't disappear totally. I learned to do my work as quickly as I could. Someday, I'd figure out a way to escape from her. And, there was still the possibility Mom would come back and rescue me from this hell she'd left me in. She'd promised she'd come back for me.

The physical pain Naomi inflicted on my body wasn't something I couldn't bear. When I'd lived with them, my two older brothers had hit me a lot, and I'd learned to not be a crybaby. Naomi wore house slippers some of the time, so she didn't hurt me as much when she kicked me with those soft moccasins on her big feet. Her kicks really hurt when she wore her leather shoes with the thick heels and hard square toes. Those black shoes needed to be heavy duty to support her big body. I think she really enjoyed kicking me with them, but she didn't wear them often, because as she complained, they made her feet sore. I guessed my yelps of pain from her punishments made her feel better about the money she kept saying my mother had cheated her out of.

The broomstick left bruises and welts. I'd gotten plenty of those when

I ran the streets of Chicago with Tommy and Ben, and we explored dangerous places together. Like most little brothers, I recovered rapidly. I even recovered from being hit by a car. I was lucky the car was barely moving when its bumper bonked my head. I prayed Naomi wouldn't break any of my bones with her heavy shoes or broomstick. I'd gotten real skinny from not having enough food to eat and that left mostly bones for her to hit. My bones were tougher than the little bit of flesh that covered them. She used the broomstick to hit my shoulders, my spine, my ribs, my hips, my wrists, my elbows, and my knuckles. I turned my face away to protect my nose and most of all I tried to shield my private parts from her punches and kicks.

Worse than the pain was the humiliation of her having such power over me. When angry, she towered over me and glared down at me like I was a worthless piece of garbage. I hated her standing over me like that. Her face filled with contempt as she kicked and punched me.

She grabbed handfuls of my hair and swung me back and forth. I felt pain the first moment my scalp gave to the pressure and pulled away from my skull and for a long time after. Her hand gripping my hair enabled her to control and direct my entire body wherever she wanted, like a cruel master jerking the chain around a dog's neck to control it.

I was ashamed of my helplessness. I was ashamed of my weakness. Nobody would do these terrible things to Tommy or Ben. They'd kill Naomi. I wanted to kill her, but I wasn't strong enough and brave enough. Although I was afraid of prison and the electric chair, I did remember from the movies the murderer's last meal always looked delicious and imagining that tray of food made me hungry.

When Naomi slapped or punched me on my ears, the pain lasted a long time. The constant ringing and droning noises in my head became the dominant sound in my world.

Many times, I didn't see the swing of the broomstick coming, but I heard it. Then I felt the pain. If there were numerous hits, sound and the pain blended together. How long the pain lasted after her hits stopped was different each time. Naomi's hits were weaker on the days she didn't feel well. Some time's they were almost a joke, but I didn't dare laugh at her. She could use her broomstick to hit me directly on my face and knock my teeth out, break and flatten my nose and gouge my eyeballs out. She might even decide to pick up a kitchen knife and cut my throat like the men at the slaughterhouses in Chicago cut the cows throats to bleed them.

I wondered if it was better to not see Naomi's hits coming at me. When I saw her hits coming towards my body, the anticipation of pain was as bad as the pain itself.

I labored at the house cleaning again and again, over and over, time after time, each and every day of my life with the devil. On my hands and knees, I washed and waxed every inch of Naomi's wood floors. I scrubbed and waxed every inch of Naomi's kitchen linoleum. I wiped clean and polished every inch of Naomi's bathroom. I wiped clean and polished every nook and cranny of Naomi's apartment, the foyer and the stairway up to my room.

Every day, I scrubbed dishes and pans in a sink that stood too high for my reach. I balanced on the tips of my toes as I scoured pans and dishes that had held better food than anything I was allowed to eat.

I hated the smell of the lye gunk Naomi forced me to use to clean her oven. As I reached deep into the oven and wiped out the lye-softened grease, I feared getting the stinking lye on my skin. I had to force the top-half of my body into her oven, so I wouldn't miss any of the lye and grease. She forced me to clean up the greasy mess from all the delicious food she baked and roasted for Emil and herself to eat.

Naomi collected the grease drippings from her cooking into coffee cans. She showed me how to make soap using grease and lye. A basement job, it frightened the hell out of me to work with lye. The stuff could eat away my skin down to my raw flesh and all the way to the bone. The nasty, poisonous fumes irritated my mouth, my nose, and my eyes terribly. I needed to make careful measurements to get the mixture just right. Since I'd have to use the lye soap for scrubbing laundry, any miscalculations I made would cause red-hot pain to my hands and arms when I labored over the scrub board doing her endless baskets of laundry.

When school was in session, I worked from early in the morning until I left for school. As soon as I got home from school, I labored until bedtime. Weekends, holidays and summer vacation, I worked from five in the morning until around seven in the evening. Then Naomi ordered me up to the solitude of my room.

Before I climbed up the stairs to my room, I sat on the floor of the foyer to take off my shoes. It was too difficult to navigate the long stairway with those loose-fitting things flopping around on my feet.

When I got up at five o'clock in the morning to begin my day, I put on my pants and tightened the belt past the original holes to the ones I made with the sharp point of a pair of scissors. I fed the too-long belt, back and forth through the loops of my big-man trousers. It took four or five rollups of the pant legs to get the length right, so I wouldn't trip and fall flat onto my face. My shirtsleeves took three or four roll-ups before I freed my hands. I carried my shoes down the stairs with me to the foyer where I put on two pairs of floppy socks and pulled my ugly shoes on. My feet still floated in those scuffed monstrosities. Sitting on the floor of the foyer, I hurried to tie my too-long shoelaces lest the renters show up and see me sitting there looking like a clown.

The door to Emil and Naomi's apartment was usually unlocked. Every day I had to force myself to approach the woman I hated more than anything else in the world.

"It's about time," Naomi barked at me as I entered the kitchen at the rear of the apartment. "What took you so long?"

I stayed silent and avoided her vicious eyes.

The dogs greeted me, one with its cautious tail wag and the other with its joyful tail wag. The Manchester terrier Manny, a sleek mostly black with brown dog, remained aloof and could be snappy. Max, the multi-colored mongrel, looked like a long-haired Basset Hound who'd borrowed a bulldog's face. He was silly-happy and always friendly. I didn't understand how he could be so joyful while living with a disgusting person like Naomi.

In a metal cage, that resembled a fancy two-story house and hung from an elaborate, metal floor stand placed in the living room, lived a canary. It was one of my duties to clean up after both the dogs and the bright-yellow, singing bird.

While Naomi prepared Emil's breakfast or dinner, I sat at the kitchen table and ate my meals. She hadn't fried eggs for me after my first day of living with her. She fed me yellow, cornmeal gruel for breakfast and a mixture of potatoes and vegetables boiled in water for dinner. I hated the turnips she forced me to eat. Many times, my food looked like scraps the dogs wouldn't even sniff at. It was better not to know exactly what she fed me. She never offered me milk. Rose told me milk was important and I'd drunk milk for the ten months I'd lived with George and Rose. I hoped that was all the milk I needed to grow up big and strong.

The cooking smells from Naomi and Emil's food made me dizzy. She fried eggs and bacon and steaks and pork chops and potatoes with onions. She baked and roasted delicious food in her oven. She liked to roll out crusts and make pies with different kinds of fillings.

The monster did force me to eat some strange things, like leftover cow's liver and fried cow brains. The brains made me puke, and she punished me with a couple vicious slaps to the side of my head and yelled at me while I cleaned up my mess.

I longed for hot dogs and tamales like my brothers and I bought from vendors along the lakefront with our shoe-shining money.

On the way to my room, I walked by Emil, who ate his dinner in the dining room. I glanced over. The pork chops he cut with his sharp knife always looked so beautiful. Naomi always fried two of them for his meal and each of the dogs got a bone. Most times, Emil left tiny bits of meat on those bones and the dogs happily gnawed the delicacies. I dreamed of getting a chance at those pork chop bones before the dogs did. Manny gave me a warning growl if I stared too hungrily at his forthcoming pork chop bone.

Emil never looked me in the eye or called me by my name. If he needed to refer to me or get my attention, he simply said, "boy." He didn't pay much attention to me at all. He made me feel I was nothing but a ghost haunting his house and he wasn't concerned at all with ghosts of enslaved children.

When I arrived home from school, Naomi made me drink a nasty liquid. A bitter drink she made by boiling some dried green leaves, she stood over me and forced me to gulp it straight down. If I hesitated, she grabbed the bottom of the glass with one hand, put her other hand on the back of my neck and forced me to swallow the brew. If I choked or spilled any, she grabbed me by my hair and slapped my face or hit me on the side of my head with her fist. Seven days a week, she forced me to drink that foul-tasting brew and the cramps it caused kept me bent over in pain.

Her nasty potion always made me rush to the toilet. There wasn't much inside of me to come out, and she yelled at me for spending too much time in her bathroom.

"Did my mother call to ask about me?"

"No, your mother didn't call to ask about you," Naomi mimicked me.

"Can I talk to her when she calls?"

"Why would she call you?"

"I don't know. If she does call, can I talk to her?"

"Didn't you hear me, you idiot? She didn't call you. She never will call you. Don't pester me with such stupid questions."

She swung her big hand towards my face. Slap!

"Ouch! I'm sorry."

"If you ever touch or go near my telephone, I'll break both of your arms!"

Walking up the stairs to my room, to be alone, the feeling never changed. Excruciating pain attacked my entire body. I was so overwhelmed, it seemed my guts had to burst out of my stomach, and my brains explode out of my skull. How could this be happening to me? Why did Mom do this to me?

I asked God to make Mom come back and rescue me. I asked God to make my brothers come running to help me when I was being beaten up on the playground or on my walk to and from school. I asked God to give me the power to kill all my enemies. I couldn't figure a way out of my terrible situation by myself. Despite all my prayers, it didn't appear God had any intention of ever helping me.

I rarely thought about Dad. I was sure my awful life happened because Dad kept saying I was a bastard. Luckily, he abandoned our family when I turned five-years-old. Probably my blond hair caused him to take Baby John to California and leave Mom and me and my other brothers behind in Chicago. I was cursed with blond hair, freckles and too much intelligence, being so different from the rest of my family is why I ended up with the monster, Naomi. I'd destroyed my own family and my own life because of the way I looked when I was born. No matter what, I didn't ever want to see my cruel bastard of a father again. My only memory of my supposed father was him being the meanest bully in the world. I hated him as much as I hated Naomi.

Chapter 12

Stacked on the floor and shelves of my closet, along with many rolls of cloth, were shoeboxes and round metal tins filled with sewing needles, pins, pincushions, spools of thread and hundreds of buttons of many sizes and colors. The lids of the tins were decorated with wonderful holiday scenes. The people pictured on the lids skated gracefully across frozen ponds, snuggled under warm blankets in horse-drawn carriages, built perfect snowmen and threw soft, fluffy snowballs at each other. Health and happiness showed on their rosy-cheeked faces. These always-smiling people then gathered indoors around brightly decorated Christmas trees with colorfully wrapped gifts stacked underneath them. Those blissful people's fireplaces glowed with brightness and warmth. Their entire world was splendid and filled with fun and games.

I divided the buttons up by size and color and used them to form large armies. My unmade bed with disarrayed blanket was a rugged, treacherous landscape where my button armies fought deadly battles.

Cannons roared.

Bullets zinged.

Bayonets stabbed.

Pow!

Blam!

Stab!

Scream!

Bleed and die!

I punched the buttons with my fists and sent them flying through the air. Mortally wounded buttons scattered over my bed and fell on my floor. I found hours of entertainment in these deadly encounters. What I enjoyed most was when I balled both of my hands into hard fists and pounded to death entire armies of my enemies on my blood-soaked battlefield. I then smashed the good button armies into oblivion and celebrated my great victory over all the buttons.

When I lived with my mother and brothers and attended Catholic school, I'd made my first confession and taken my first communion. I barely understood what was happening and was frightened by the religious rituals and by being in the huge cathedral where we worshipped. I didn't like any of the boring religious lessons taught in school, but I did fear ending up in the raging inferno of hell. Most of all, I feared the violent tempers of the sisters who taught at the Catholic school. I forgot all that religion stuff after Dad abandoned our family and we eventually switched to public schools. Like my older brothers, I didn't know or care about books. My oldest brother, Tommy, liked to say, "They ain't gonna make me read any fucking books." I didn't like any of the books I was forced to read at school, and when I had a choice, I wanted to read comic books. Mostly, I wanted to be out on the streets of Chicago with my older brothers.

I was terribly bored in my prison cell of a room and desperate for any distraction from the solitude. I flipped through the two books in my nightstand, the Bible and Pilgrims Progress. It was a struggle to read Pilgrim's Progress, but I kept at it. The Bible was easier, and I forced myself to keep reading the holy book.

"In the beginning, God created the heaven and the earth," I read, from the book that didn't have pictures to help me understand the story. "And the earth was without form, and void; and darkness was upon the face of the deep. And the spirit of God moved upon the face of the waters."

I read on and on about God's greatness. I didn't understand all the words, but the story impressed me. Ahead of me lay a lot of reading to get up to the present day and the world I now lived in. The "begats" were boring but reading about the evil that arose again and again in the world helped me better understand why there were people like my cruel father and the monster, Naomi. Life wasn't supposed to be easy.

"As I walked through the wilderness of this world," I read from Pilgrim's Progress, "I lighted on a certain place where was a den and laid me down in that place to sleep; and as I slept, I dreamed a dream."

I understood sleeping in the safety of a den, except it wasn't safe if a large, wild animal came in to attack you. Then the den would be a death trap. My room was like the den in the story. My room was safe when I was alone, but it became a terrifying trap when Naomi climbed the stairway, opened my door and invaded my small space.

I understood having a dream. I had lots of dreams, but too many of my dreams had me sliding towards the edge of the earth.

The sky filled with towering black clouds and hurricane winds tossed me about and pushed me towards the abyss, an endless ocean of huge, dark waves. I clawed at the crumbling edge of a cliff to keep from falling thousands of feet to my death. Many times, I fell and sank into icy, cold waters. Drowning woke me up. I struggled to stay awake and avoid the nightmare's return. Eventually, I succumbed to sleep, and the dream continued. *I hung onto the edge of the earth, but my hands and arms grew tired, and I dropped into what was now a fire filled abyss. I tumbled over and over until I reached the inferno. I was trapped and surrounded by flames that burned the flesh from my body, and I turned into a red-hot cinder that floated away in a howling wind.*

I woke up feverish and sweating and thrashing to be free from my blankets. Relief surged through me as I checked all my body parts and discovered no part of me was burned to a crisp.

The guy in Pilgrim's Progress didn't wake up. His story was a dream that went on and on without end. I could only read so much about him before my brain ached.

I liked the window in my room. I'd look out onto the avenue below and watch life happen. I watched the children at play and listened to their laughs and shouts.

I didn't have a chair in my room, and the radiator was directly below the window, so I had to stand to look out at the world. In winter, the radiator was too hot to touch so I couldn't lean against it like I did in summer. When steam surged through the radiator, it clanked and hissed loudly. I was scared it would suddenly explode, and flying chunks of metal would rip me to shreds, and the steam would cook what was left. If I got bored of standing, I sat on the floor and looked up at the waving treetops and the clouds racing across the sky. I remembered the promise in the bible of going to heaven if I prayed to God for forgiveness of my sins. I prayed and waited for the radiator to explode and for the explosion to end my life. I'd fly up into the deep-blue sky and be with God forever. Everyone would regret how badly they'd treated me when I was alive.

I lay on my bed and thought about food. I imagined plates filled with fried pork chops, fried potatoes, and fried onions or roast beef and mashed potatoes with gravy. I'd fill my stomach with banana cream pies, chocolate cakes and gallons of strawberry ice cream and drink bottles of root beer, orange soda, and coca cola. I'd stuff candy bars, cream-filled cupcakes and buttered popcorn in my mouth. Every morning, I'd eat fried eggs, bacon and pancakes soaked with maple syrup. I'd thrill with anticipation as I pulled the wrappers off Fudgesicles, Creamsicles, and Eskimo pies.

I fantasized about going outside to play. I'd be in gunfights, trade comic books and shoot marbles. I'd fish from the piers at lakefront parks and go to the matinee movies with Tommy and Ben. I'd collect deposit bottles, dive for golf balls and hustle on the streets for money. I really missed the movies, the fishing and the wading in Lake Michigan. Once I was free from this awful place and no longer a slave to Naomi, I'd be part of that wonderful and exciting world again.

I lay on my bed and stared at the ceiling. Different images appeared in the patterns of the plaster. I saw faces up there. I saw faces of all the people I remembered from my childhood. I saw Mom's sweet, loving face. I saw the laughing faces of my brothers. I also saw scary faces. I saw Dad's cruel, mocking face. I saw growling, foam-mouthed mongrel dogs, arch-backed hissing alley cats, and red-eyed scurrying rats.

I felt better if I hid completely under the covers. In darkness, it was easier to imagine a better world than the one I now lived in. I saw myself as Tarzan swinging from tree to tree in the jungle, barely avoiding the sharp claws and gnashing teeth of leaping, raging lions. I was Roy Rogers astride a galloping Trigger, cleaning up the Wild West, shooting all the outlaws with my pair of six-guns.

My feelings about Mom confused me. There was so much I loved about her. I loved the sound of her voice when she was cheerful. I loved how she looked when she wore makeup and was dressed up in her best clothes. I loved how she held me close to her body, and the smell of her perfume. I was losing the sense of how being close to Mom felt. I wanted to believe she'd be terribly sorry if I got sick and died. She'd sob gallons of tears because she wouldn't ever be able to hug me again.

Or had she quit loving me altogether? Is that why she got rid of me?

Would Mom or anyone be sorry if I died? Naomi would only care I wouldn't be around to be her house slave. She'd miss having me to scream at and to beat. Emil might notice I was gone. He might even say my name at my funeral.

"That boy had a name," he'd say. "His name was Mickey. He was a real, living, breathing boy. He was a hard-working boy. I feel terrible I barely noticed Mickey's existence. I shouldn't have let Naomi be so cruel to him."

"We rarely saw that boy except when he was shoveling snow or doing other outside work," the neighbors chorused. "Everything seemed fine with him. Naomi said his own mother didn't want him. His mother offered him to strangers who might have been evil people. He was so lucky a caring, God-fearing person like Naomi gave him a first-class home."

"His own mother put an advertisement in the newspaper to get rid of him," Naomi intoned. "That unwanted boy was lucky I took him into my house. So many bad things could have happened to him out on the dangerous streets of Chicago. He'd probably have died much sooner than he did. His mother was a filthy, lying whore. That skinny bitch cheated me out of my ten dollars a week."

"God bless you, Naomi," everybody agreed. "That boy was so lucky you took him into your lovely home. You're a fine, God-fearing person. It's a shame his rotten mother cheated you out of the money she'd promised to pay you."

Rage boiled inside of me. I hated Naomi, and I hated Mom. But, like Naomi said all the time, I was an ungrateful slum boy. I was a bad slum boy. I faked more pain than was real, so she'd stop hitting me. I faked my submission to her. I secretly wanted to injure and maybe kill her. I cheated her when I stole time for myself, when I paused, rested, or avoided work when she wasn't watching me closely. Because my mother was a lying, cheating bitch, I owed Naomi my labor. But I defied Naomi by becoming a groveling, but cunning sneak. I stole tiny bits of food I wasn't entitled to. I was exactly like the stray dogs that sulked from garbage can to garbage can in the stinking alleys of Chicago.

Despite how brutally she tried, Naomi hadn't broken me completely.

Would I realize when I was completely broken? If I didn't run away or kill Naomi soon, would she beat me down to nothing? I needed to run away. I could join a band of outlaws and roam the countryside with them. I'd fit in well with a gang of desperados. I was already an expert thief.

My bed rose into the air and pitched back and forth like a scrap of wood on a violent sea. Wobbling wildly, my bed rose faster and faster towards the ceiling. I was going to be crushed and killed. I crawled to the very edge of my mattress. I looked over the side. It was a long drop to the floor. If I fell, I'd break all my bones and die. The bed pitched me forward, and I tumbled over the side. I grabbed the blanket and barely held on with my fingertips. I slipped further and further downward. The floor turned into a dark, tossing ocean. I clawed and clawed back up the side of the bed, but I grew tired. I lost my grip. I fell and fell and fell. I turned over and over and over. I landed on the surface of an icy, cold sea. I tried to swim, but I couldn't swim. The water sucked me under, and I sank deeper and deeper and deeper. I couldn't breathe—.

I woke up on the floor of my room. Every part of my body ached. I slowly stood up and stretched. I walked around my room. My body began to work again. None of my parts appeared broken. Damn. It wouldn't be as easy to kill myself as I'd imagined and hoped it would be.

Chapter 13

For winter wear, Naomi handed me a well-worn, faded-orange color, old woman's cloth-coat that had a brown and white, fake-fur collar. The fake-fur trimmed sleeve-ends didn't reach far enough to cover my skinny wrists. I struggled to button the too-small coat over my man clothes, which bunched up under my dreadful, new piece of clothing.

"Do I have to wear this?" I wanted to cry. I wanted to puke.

"What do you think, stupid?"

"I don't really need a coat." I fought against my urge to scream.

"Don't argue with me. I don't need a sick kid around here. If you don't wear a coat, you'll catch pneumonia and probably die."

I watched her face redden. Her hands clenched into fists. I backed up to stay out of her hitting range. I bumped into the wall behind me, and my retreat was blocked.

"Do I really have to wear this coat?" It would be better to die than wear that awful coat.

"Yes, you do! Quit arguing with me, you idiot!"

I shriveled up into a smaller target and cringed sideways, but she didn't attempt to hit me. She was feeling too much of her own pain. Her fat body moved slowly and awkwardly when she wasn't feeling well.

I didn't have galoshes to wear on the deep-snow days.

"Take these nylon stockings," Naomi ordered. "You can pull them up over your shoes and pant legs."

I took the stockings from her. One was a darker color than the other, and both showed several jagged runs in them. Once again, I wanted to scream, and I felt the need to puke.

"Take these rubber bands," she ordered. "Pull them over the stockings close to the top of the nylons. The rubber bands will hold the stockings in place."

I reluctantly took the rubber bands she handed to me.

"The stockings and rubber bands will work fine," she said. "You won't have any excuse for getting your shoes and pants wet from the snow."

I held the nylons in one hand and the rubber bands in the other. My stomach churned with sourness. My head wanted to explode into a million pieces.

When it was time to leave for school, I sat on the bottom step of the back porch and pulled the nylons up over my shoes. I pulled the rubber bands up over the nylons. I stood up and forced myself to walk along the walkway through the backyard. I pushed through the back gate and turned left into the alley.

I had the choice of traversing the rubble-strewn, vacant field directly across the alley behind our garage or walking several blocks up the alley. Both routes were deep in snow. Usually, I took whichever path I sensed was safest from bullies that day. As soon as I was past any chance of Naomi seeing me, I took the nylons and rubber bands off and stuffed them deep into my coat pockets. The old-woman coat was horror enough.

I hadn't avoided all my tormentors.

"That's a woman's coat, you fucking idiot."

"You look so stupid, you freak.

"Are you a queer or just a retard?"

Snowballs peppered me. I hunched over and stared at the snow-covered ground ahead of me as I tried to walk faster.

The knee-deep snow made it impossible to run from my enemies. The snow packed into my shoes from the top, and I struggled with the extra weight.

My schoolmates created a new game that started when I got close to school. Groups of kids watched as I stepped cautiously across large patches of icy ground. Someone would sneak up behind me and give a shove. With my feet totally beyond my control, I fell on my skinny ass. Damn, that hurt. I struggled back to a standing position. Another push. Another fall on the slippery surface. I'd catch myself bare-handed, and bits of gravel and ice got embedded in my palms.

I slipped and slid on the ice, again, and again.

Laughter surrounded me.

"He's a clumsy old woman."

I had nowhere to hide. I crawled deeper and deeper into my rotten, hate-filled self.

At school, I sat on the front steps and emptied the snow out of my clodhoppers before going inside. I clomped through the hallways. I clomped up the stairways. I clomped into the classroom.

"Listen to the gimp. Ha. Ha. Ha."

When I sat at my desk, I slipped my shoes off so my frozen feet could thaw out and dry. They never completely warmed up. After school, I put the nylons back on as soon as I was out of sight of my classmates.

"Why are your shoes and pant legs wet?" Naomi grabbed me by my hair. She twisted and pulled my hair to force me closer to her stinking body. She slapped my face. I saw an explosion of stars and brilliant streaks of colors

"Ouch. I'm sorry. The nylons leaked."

"They wouldn't have leaked if you'd put them on right, stupid." She kicked me on my skinny ankle. A sharp stab of pain radiated up my leg. "Put dry pants on. Hang those wet clothes in the basement and get to work."

She released my hair; I cringed and groveled away from her.

I walked down the back stairs to the basement. I put on my other pair of oversized pants and set my shoes close to the furnace to dry. I found a pair of mismatched dry socks and pulled them on. I hung up my wet pants and made several trips to the back porch, where baskets of laundry waited for me. I settled in close to the wash tubs and labored over the scrub board. I scrubbed the laundry viciously, bruising and bloodying my knuckles on the board in the process. I doused the water-laden linens again and again in the rinse water tub. When I wrung water from the thick material, I imagined my hands around Naomi's fat neck. I was wringing the life out of her. That thought enabled me to squeeze the water out of the laundry much easier.

After I finished my work in the basement, I climbed the stairway to the back porch and entered the kitchen where Naomi loomed. I sat down at the table to eat my boiled turnips and potatoes.

"Did you finish all your work?"

"Yes, ma'am."

"As soon as you're done eating, wash the dishes."

"Yes, ma'am."

"Don't talk with food in your mouth."

"Yes, ma'am."

"Don't talk back!"

"Sorry, ma'am."

I finished eating and washed the dishes. "I'm done with the dishes."

"Go up to your room."

"Yes, ma'am."

The man who rented the spare bedroom in Naomi and Emil's apartment was a complete mystery to me. He arrived home every day around six-thirty in the evening and said few words beyond: "Hello." "Yes, it was cold today." and "Yes, I'm feeling fine." He used the bathroom, next to his room, said goodnight, entered his room and closed the door behind him. He stayed quietly in that room until early morning.

All a person could see from his one window was our narrow concrete walkway, a short wooden fence and the brown-brick wall of the two-story building next door. I was glad it wasn't my room. At least in my room, the window looked out on Hamlin Avenue. I couldn't understand him willingly being alone in that room all those long, boring hours. He was free to come and go whenever he wanted. He was free to go to dinner or to a movie. He was free to eat hot dogs, candy bars and buttered popcorn. He was free to drink lots of sodas.

He always wore a suit, so I guess he had an important job. With his fat body, balding head and pasty face, I couldn't imagine him with a woman friend. For sure, nobody like my mother would want to be around him. She liked to laugh and go out to dinner with noisy men. There wasn't any way she'd marry someone like him.

He was gone most weekends so something fun might be happening in his life. In that way, he was better off than me. I spent every weekend of my life working, and the hours I wasn't working, I was confined to the solitude of my room.

The boarder didn't look at me like he was interested in looking at and touching young boy penises. I appreciated that.

Some of the days I climbed the stairs up to my room, the only thing I wanted to do was crawl into the bed, hide under the covers and pray I would die.

No matter how many times I prayed for death, I always woke up to Naomi. Why didn't God hear me?

At school, I faced constant bullying by the meanest children. Even some of the nicer kids couldn't resist taunting me. I hated going to school as much as I hated being around Naomi.

I dreaded being called to the front of the classroom to stand in front of my smirking classmates.

"Clomp, clomp and clomp."

I had to avoid the feet sticking out in the narrow aisle intended to trip me and send me sprawling on my face. I walked slowly, but those tripping feet easily got me.

I staggered forward and fell to my knees. I grabbed onto the edge of a desk to pull myself up; a fist pounded my hand. Most of the boys punched my ribs or stomach if I touched them during my stagger. Eventually, I reached the front of the classroom.

There I stood, dressed in my raggedy, old-man clothes amidst a chorus of laughter.

"Quiet children!" the teacher yelled. She looked at me with ever-expanding irritation. I knew she hated me. I made her job more difficult because I was odd, and I made the children in class react. My appearance and mannerisms upset children and adults.

I hoped and prayed that someday, I'd be huge and powerful, and I could kill every one of my tormentors. I'd kill everyone in the world. I'd grab them by their throats and smash them against the ground as I choked them to death. I'd rip their heads from their bodies and watch their blood spurt from the tops of their necks.

Chapter 14

Ryerson School staged a Thanksgiving play about the Pilgrims sharing a feast with their redskin neighbors. The hours I spent struggling through the Bible and Pilgrims Progress had improved my reading skill, and I had a strong voice. A sympathetic teacher selected me for the part in the play that had the most words to say. During rehearsals, I walked across the wooden stage in my oversized shoes. The auditorium resonated with the clump each step I took.

Each time I lifted up and put down my feet, the clump brought laughter from all the children on the stage.

"Mickey," the teacher asked kindly. "Can you get a different pair of shoes to wear?"

"I'll try, ma'am."

I relayed the teacher's request to Naomi.

As I anticipated, Naomi didn't respond well. "Tell that teacher she can buy you new shoes after she pays me all the money your lying bitch of a mother didn't send me. You're an ungrateful bastard!"

She grabbed me by my hair and twisted, then slapped me on my ear.

When would I learn not to listen to or trust any grownups? Damn. I was stupid.

The next day I walked across the stage during practice.

Clomp.

Clomp.

Clomp.

Laughter cascaded from the children. Once again, I'd interrupted the rehearsal.

"When will you have different shoes, Mickey?" Now, this kind teacher sounded frustrated with me. It wasn't my fault I was a freak, but everyone acted like it was. Back when I was on the streets with my brothers, people thought I was a tough, bad boy. Now I was just an oddball sissy.

"I don't have better shoes to wear, ma'am. I'm sorry."

"I'm sorry too, Mickey. You need to take another part. The noise you make when you walk is too distracting. I'm really sorry."

The teacher gave me a small part, where I didn't have to move at all. I only had a couple of words to shout out. I guessed I wasn't going to be a famous stage actor. I walked like a shackled convict, whose spirit had been totally broken by his burden of leg chains.

Naomi cut my hair with me sitting on a stool in the kitchen. I struggled to sit up straight and remain still. Always in a hurry when she barbered, she caught the edges of my ears between the dull blades of her sewing scissors and squeezed. I jerked to escape from the sharp pain. I was terrified she'd cut off a chunk of my ear, and that bloody piece of ear would fall on the floor, and she'd force me to remain sitting on the stool bleeding to death.

"Hold still," she screamed. "Cutting your hair reminds me of scything down wheat when I was a young girl."

She jabbed the sharp point of her scissors into the fat part of my ear. I felt blood trickle down my neck. I started to raise my hand, desperate to check the damage she'd inflicted on me.

"I said to hold still, stupid. Do you want me to cut off your whole ear and throw it into the garbage?"

She poked my scalp several times with the sharp point of her scissors. Blood bubbled up from the wounds. Her garlicky, oniony breath choked me. She flapped her flabby arms up and down like an angry chicken. The odor from her hairy, wrinkled underarms gagged me. The monster relentlessly chopped away at my hair. She poked the point of the scissors into my damaged scalp again and again. Blood seeped from my wounds and inched its way down my face. I was terrified. I cringed and pulled away.

"HOLD STILL, STUPID!"

I didn't care how freaky I'd look. I needed to get away from the monster and her deadly scissors. But I couldn't escape.

Finally, she finished butchering my hair. "Now, clean up this mess, stupid."

When I walked to school, I couldn't hide my butchered hair or my scabby scalp.

"Hey, look at that mess on his head."

"Somebody used a lawnmower on his head."

"You look like one of those people in the newsreels at the movies. You look like one of those Jews from a Nazi death camp."

"You're right. He looks just like a Jew from a concentration camp."

"That's the stupidest haircut I've ever seen."

"Whoever gave you that haircut really hated you."

Naomi forgot to leave enough hair on my head to grab onto and twist when she was angry. Now she grabbed me by one of my wounded ears. I feared she'd twist and pull my ears right off my head. That would make a terrible, bloody mess. Without ears, I'd look more freakish than I already did, and everybody'd hate me more than they already did.

Seeking help, I read from the bible. I read about the suffering of Jesus Christ. I prayed to Jesus. "Please, Jesus. Help me. Stop my hair from growing." I guess the Devil overheard my pleas and he had more power than Jesus because my hair grew faster.

"Come over here, stupid. It's time for another haircut. Your ugly hair grows faster than the weeds in my flower garden. Climb on the stool.

And you'd better stay still this time, or you'll really be sorry!"

"Aaaaaah!" My screams of terror came from deep inside of me, and the monster didn't hear them.

I crawled deeper and deeper into the black pit down inside of myself, but I couldn't escape from Naomi and her damn scissors.

Chapter 15

I woke up to a gloomy morning and stared at the ceiling. Terrifying nightmares dominated most of my night but, I had one joyous dream of many gifts, of toys, Christmas cookies covered with candy sprinkles, ham and sweet potatoes baked with brown sugar and hugs instead of hits. My craving for a loving and generous holiday made my stomach ache and forced tears to well up into my eyes.

I forced myself out from under my blankets and sat on the edge of my bed dreading what most likely lay ahead.

Outside my window was a gray, low-hanging overcast that made me feel even gloomier. A light snow fell, but street lamps barely illuminated the white powder. Across the street, a solitary, holiday wreath peeked from behind a frosted-over window. Along the whole block, only two red and green lights twinkled. I wanted to jump back into bed and find refuge in the blackness under the covers, but my fear of Naomi's violent temper spurred me to get dressed and trudge downstairs to face reality.

Naomi and Emil sat in the front parlor with a small, but colorfully decorated Christmas tree placed on a corner table. Underneath the tree were a couple of presents they'd already opened. The two dogs lay close to the radiators and wagged a greeting to me. Music like you'd hear in a grand cathedral soared from the radio. The smell of fried ham and eggs, potatoes and buttered toast lingered in the air.

"So, you finally got up," Naomi growled.

"I'm sorry."

Emil looked like he wanted to speak but checked himself.

"There's work to be done before you eat your breakfast," she declared.

"I know."

"Won't you ever quit talking back?" Her anger rose quickly and without warning.

Emil retreated into his shell and ignored my existence.

I descended to the semi-dark basement to do my furnace work. I broke up clinkers, scooped out ashes, and shoveled fresh coal from the bin. Soon the fire was blazing anew.

With my ugly, old-woman coat and a pair of Emil's black-rubber galoshes on, I marched outdoors to shovel the several inches of new snow that accumulated overnight. I used the sharp edge of the scoop-shovel to scrape away the layers of ice that coated the front porch steps and the walkways. My feet tingled from the iced-over concrete. I wiped my dripping nose on the coat sleeve.

Shoveling the deep snow was tougher when it turned slushy, and I could barely lift it.

After I finished outdoors, I returned to the basement to thaw my hands by the furnace. I was tempted to open the furnace door and stick my numb, red fingers directly into the red-hot flames.

Finally, I could eat my bowl of cold, yellow cornmeal and slice of dry toast. The caged canary sing along with the Christmas music on the radio. In a low voice, I sang along with him. I washed the dishes and pans from Naomi and Emil's delicious breakfast of ham and eggs and fried potatoes.

My Christmas day chores took only a few hours.

Naomi examined the dishes. "You're done for today. You can go back up to your room."

Foolishly, I longed for an invitation to stay and for a surprise gift to appear. I really wanted to own a set of the plastic Cowboys who fired their six-guns and a set of their enemies, the Redskins who pulled taut the arrows in their bows. I also imagined a dozen of the gallant, galloping horses they both sat upon.

"Thanks."

"Go on," she ordered.

Emil sat in his favorite chair and read the newspaper. As usual, he didn't look at me as I passed through the parlor. The dogs picked up their heads and eyed me, but they didn't give up their warm spots next to the radiators. At least Manny and Max acknowledged my existence, my only reminder that I was a living, breathing person.

I walked back up the stairs to the second floor and into my room. Slamming the door was my protest that nobody ever saw or understood. I lay down on the floor next to the door to the renter's place. As I spied on them, I stayed as quiet as humanly possible. I always feared the wood flooring would creak and reveal my presence as a sneaky spy. I listened closely to what was happening during their Christmas celebration. Four different voices talked excitedly to sounds of tearing and crinkling holiday wrapping paper.

"Thank you, so much!"

"That's exactly what I needed!"

"This is perfect!"

"A Merry Christmas to everyone!"

On their radio, Gene Autry sang "Rudolph the Red-Nosed Reindeer." I stood up and walked over and looked out my window. The overcast had lifted, and the day had brightened. Hamlin Avenue glowed with festive holiday lights and the new snowfall. Across the street, a family clambered out of a just-parked car. The parents and their two excited children carried presents as they walked up the front steps to a house. One of the kids rang the doorbell, and the front door opened. The beaming-with-happiness people all smiled, hugged and kissed as they were swept inside, closing the door behind them. I didn't want to think about all the happiness inside that home.

I crawled into my bed. I hid completely under the covers and curled into a tight ball. There were many more hours left in this terrible Christmas day. There were many more hours of being alone ahead of me. I didn't believe I could live through more of the loneliness that ruled my life. As hungry as I was, I didn't want to go downstairs to eat whatever the monster would allow me for my Christmas dinner. I didn't want to be anywhere near her.

I now clearly understood the truth. There were weeks and months of being alone ahead of me. This Christmas day, I didn't see how I could survive my daily torture of solitude. It was too much for me.

Why did my mother leave me with this horrible woman? How could she walk away and leave me behind? I'd stood before her sniveling and shedding tears, but she still abandoned me. What was so horribly wrong with me?

My birthday was a month and a half after Christmas. I was nearly ten-years-old.

I was falling down a black hole. I was turning over and over in the darkness. I couldn't see a bottom to the hole. I feared I'd fall forever.

Suddenly, I was lying at the bottom of the hole. I was lying on a cold, concrete floor. It was a small, dark space I was trapped in.

A small sliver of light shone faintly from under a thick, steel door.

I felt around the surface of the door searching for a doorknob. I couldn't find one. I tried to see under the door, but the space between the bottom of the door and the floor was too narrow to see anything except the thin sliver of light.

The sound was faint, but I heard cheerful voices on the other side of the door.

"HELLO," I shouted. "HELLO!"

No one answered me.

I pushed against the door with my shoulder, but the door wouldn't open.

I clawed at the surface of the door trying to get a grip on the cold, steel surface with the tips of my fingers. The door might open inward towards me.

I couldn't get a grip.

The space between the cold, steel door and the cold concrete wall was narrow enough for me to lean against the concrete wall and press my feet against the steel door.

I pushed against the door with the bottoms of my bare feet.

I pushed.

I pushed really hard.

I was straining, and I was screaming.

"HELLO!"

I grew tired and took a rest.

Sitting alone in the darkness, I cried.

The little sliver of light taunted me.

The happy voices on the other side of the door taunted me.

I was frantic now.

I was sobbing.

Once again, I pushed against the door with all my strength.

I screamed.

"HELP ME."

"PLEASE HELP ME!"

I startled awake. It was dark except for the eerie glow of the streetlights that showed through my window. My eyes followed the shifting spotlights thrown across my ceiling and my walls by the occasional passing cars or trucks. The nightstand clock hands pointed to three o'clock. I'd slept through the rest of Christmas day. I'd missed Christmas dinner and my once favorite holiday was behind me.

I was still alone. I was alone in this bed. I was alone in this room. I was alone in this world. I was alone in my life. I was deep in a pit of aloneness I couldn't escape from. Mom must rescue me before another Christmas happens. Please, Mom. I can't stand to be alone anymore.

Chapter 16

My stomach rumbled from hunger, but there was nothing for me to eat. I tensed every muscle in my body until I felt like a solid mass of stone. I wanted to become a carnival sideshow freak known as the solid-stone boy. Long lines of people would walk by and stare and look me in the eye and shake their heads with pity. I'd be the biggest attraction on the midway. I'd be the abandoned boy who, except for his heart and his head, had turned himself into a solid slab of stone. I'd be world famous as the solid-stone boy.

The mercy of sleep enveloped me again.

I ran towards a distant Christmas tree with many presents stacked under it. It was surrounded by children waving their arms and laughing. I desperately wanted to join them. I ran faster. I tripped and fell. I turned over and over and rolled underneath the Christmas tree. There were no decorations hanging from its branches anymore, and all the presents were gone. The tree had changed into a needleless skeleton of barren branches. Off in the distance, the crowd of laughing children were running away with my gifts. The children clutched the ornaments, the presents and green needles from the tree with their large, gnarly hands. I stood and ran after them as fast as I could. I called out. "Wait for me!" I tripped again. I landed on my face and blood gushed from my smashed nose. I screamed, "Wait for me!" I struggled to my feet. I tried to run, but I couldn't move forward. I couldn't see or hear the children anymore. The ground had become a conveyor belt that was pulling me backwards. I couldn't escape this terrifying new danger.

I fell backwards off the conveyor belt and plummeted head over heels into a terrifying abyss of howling, storm-tossed ocean.

"Mom!" I screamed. Towering black waves crashed down on me. I sank under the ice- cold water. I couldn't breathe.

I startled awake again. I'd pushed my covers off, and I was shivering from the cold. I pulled my covers back over me, and I scrunched my body into as tight a mass as possible.

I told myself I needed to be stronger. I needed to quit being afraid of everyone and everything in the world.

"Why didn't you come down to eat last night?" Naomi chided me as I entered the kitchen.

"I wasn't hungry."

"Well, stupid. When you're hungry enough, you'll eat."

"Yes, ma'am."

I descended to the cold, shadowy basement and did my furnace work.

At the kitchen table, the yellow gruel in front of me looked the same as it did every morning of my terrible life with Naomi. I ate every last bit of it. As I ate, I stared at the sink stacked full of dirty pans and dishes waiting for me to scrub them clean. Naomi and Emil had eaten lots of delicious food on Christmas day.

I lay down on the floor of my room and slithered up close against the door to the stairway. As one of the renters ascended the stairway, I listened to their footsteps. They reached the landing outside my door. He opened the apartment door and called out to his wife.

"Hello, honey! I'm home."

At other times, it was she who climbed up the stairway, opened the door and called into the apartment to him, "I'm home, dear!"

Many times, they climbed the stairs together conversing quietly or struggled with bags of groceries as they unlocked their door. It always scared me when they paused too long on the landing. Did they know I was in my room, lying on my floor with my ear to my door spying on them? I stayed as quiet as possible. My worst fear was they'd detect my presence next to the door. They'd hear me breathing. They'd hear my heart beating. They'd hear me thinking. I was horribly fearful they'd say something to me through the door. To be caught spying on them would destroy one of my favorite pastimes. But they didn't seem cruel enough to do that. I wondered if they knew and enjoyed the spying game as much as I did.

My shame at my situation as a slave to Naomi was bearable only, if I alone, knew the complete, humiliating truth.

I imagined I was one of the terrified victims in the murder movies. I hid silently in the dark shadows and shook with fear as I awaited discovery by the stalking murderer. Their footsteps came closer and closer to me. My nerves vibrated, and I choked back a scream. Suddenly, the murderer discovered me. They grabbed me by my hair, pulled me close and slit my throat from ear to ear with their razor-sharp knife. They threw me to the ground, and all my blood drained from my body. I was a dead slave boy.

My imaginings of discovery and death were exactly like the times I heard Naomi's heavy bulk climbing the stairway to my room. Tightly gripping the handrail, she relentlessly pulled herself up each step. Her house slippers didn't make much noise, but the weight of her big body strained the structure of the stairway. Wood creaked and groaned. Nails screamed in agony. Total collapse seemed imminent. Short of breath, the monster wheezed and gasped for air, and often stopped to rest. I hoped the beast would fall over backwards and go thumping down the staircase until she reached the bottom, dead as a slaughterhouse cow that had been hit over its head with a sledgehammer. That would be a wonderful sound to hear and I'd celebrate wildly.

The creaks stopped as she gained the landing outside my door. I heard her catch her breath. I stood and stepped back away from the door. I watched the doorknob turn. The door opened. There she stood, revealed in all her huge, ugly meanness. Her face was flushed from the exertion of the climb. I'd backed up as far as possible across my room until I was trapped against a wall.

My room was really my prison cell. Naomi was the merciless prison warden. She'd climbed up the stairway to lead me to the gallows to be hung or to the electric chair to be fried to a crisp. But I was supposed to enjoy a delicious last meal before they killed me. There wasn't any way I'd get a generous last meal from the stingy hag, Naomi. Damn her to hell.

"How come your bed isn't made?" she demanded. She approached me. "What are you doing with my buttons? Goddamn you. Put my stuff back in the closet. Pick your socks up off the floor, you slob. This isn't a slum like where you came from. Can't you ever learn, you stupid clod?"

She balled up her fists and lumbered towards me. The sound of voices drifted through the door from the renter's front room. She stopped and listened. She turned toward the door to the renter's place. She looked frustrated. I sensed her rage boiling over. She turned back to glare at me.

"You clean up this room, you pig." Her voice was low and harsh. Her breathing was ragged, her face pale and her hands trembled as she turned to leave. Was she going to fall over dead? I needed to pray harder that she would. She slammed my cell's door shut behind her.

I relaxed.

I listened for the bouncing sounds of her body as she stumbled, fell and tumbled down the stairs. I prayed for the loud wail of her death scream.

It didn't come.

Why not, God? Why not?

Cleaning the entry vestibule and the stairway to the second floor was one of my constantly repeated duties. Carpet ran up the middle of the stairway, with varnished wood on each side of the colorfully patterned material. I swept the carpet with a broom. On my hands and knees, I wiped away any dust on the wood with a damp rag. The renters often appeared while I was cleaning. He stood tall and thick of body, always neatly dressed and well groomed. She stood tall and thin of body and, like him, was always well groomed and neatly dressed. She smelled of perfume that reminded me of Mom. Thinking about Mom made my gut ache.

"How are you, son?" a deep male or soft female voice asked. I imagined a smile on their faces. They were always friendly.

"I'm fine, sir," or "I'm fine, ma'am," I muttered quietly. I kept my head bowed and my gaze on their feet. Deeply ashamed, I didn't want to look them in the eye. When they were far enough away, and I sensed they weren't watching me, I glanced up. Mostly, I saw their backs or quick flashes of their faces. If they caught me looking at them, I turned away. I hated that moment. I didn't want anyone to see me as a real, living person who allowed himself to be used and abused as a slave. I didn't need looks of pity from anyone.

Chapter 17

School had let out for the day, and I hadn't fled fast enough to escape the after-school gauntlet. Damn my oversized clodhoppers. I'd been tackled and was lying flat on my back on the blacktop. A big, cruel kid sat on my chest. He grabbed a handful of my raggedy hair and banged my head against the hard, gravely surface of the playground. My eyes watered from the concussion and my ears distorted the voices of the excited children who surrounded us and cheered on my attacker.

"You fucking freak."

"Stop it," a girl's voice yelled. "Leave him alone."

I felt uplifted by her voice of sympathy and her plea for mercy for raggedy, freaky me.

He threw a few punches to my face. I covered up with my bony arms, but his hard fist got through to my chin and my lips.

When he'd tired of punching me, he got up off me, slapped his hands together and grunted, "freak," to signal his victory. I rolled onto my side and curled into a tight ball. Once again, I could taste my own blood. "Why don't you fight back, you retard," he said, his voice dripping with disgust. Muttered insults scorched my ears as I lay silent on my side, my knees drawn up to my chest. Someone kicked me in my back. A lightning bolt of pain traveled along my spine. I straightened slightly to relieve the throbbing agony. Then, I lay quietly. The circle of children broke apart. Their footsteps and voices grew distant. Time passed. Sweet bird songs magically filled the silence.

Many people thought I was a mute. I'd learned that silence was the best way to end the attacks. What the hell, I'd no idea what I should say. Either I had to fight back, or I had to keep quiet. I'd lost the will to fight back. Dealing with Naomi's sudden and vicious assaults had trained me well in the art of accepting punishment.

Slowly, I got up and looked around. I was alone on the playground. I was still able to walk, so I shuffled home to face Naomi. My head ached inside and out. I reached up and felt blood matted on the back of my scalp. I wiped blood from my split lip. My back still hurt from the kick and my jaw ached from the punches.

"Why are you so late?" Naomi yelled. She grabbed me by my hair and slapped me on my sore jaw. She released my hair when she felt the moistness of my bloody scalp.

"You're bleeding. Don't get blood on my floor. Why didn't you say something?" She pushed and pulled me across the kitchen. "What's wrong with you? Come over here to the sink."

She turned the cold water on full. She pushed my head down under the faucet with her heavy, rough hands. My blood, mixed with the ice-cold water, streamed down the sides of my face and filled my mouth. I was choking to death. She suddenly let go of me. My head popped up and hit the faucet opening and sprayed water on the beast.

"Goddamn," she yelled. "Hold still, you idiot."

She grabbed the back of my neck. She pushed down, applying a viselike grip on my neck as she rubbed more water onto my wound. Watery blood whirled around the sink and swirled down the drain. I banged my head on the faucet again as I tried to avoid drowning.

"Watch what you're doing." She grabbed an old, stained towel and roughly dried my wounded head. "Stand up straight now, stupid."

I struggled to stand up straight. Her arms flailed, and her elbow hit my ear. I feared she'd rip my ear completely from my head.

"You're going to be fine," she said as she pushed me away. "Can't you stay out of trouble?"

I almost fell to my knees when she pushed me away, but somehow, I stayed on my feet. I regained a semblance of balance.

"Get to your work now. You're wearing out my patience."

"I'm sorry."

"I don't want to hear sorry. You're as worthless as a filthy, stray dog from the alley."

All throughout the long winter, I'd spent many hours tending the furnace, but recently that task got easier. A stoker, a recent purchase squeezed out of Naomi's tight purse, now fed the coal into the furnace. Refilling the stoker from the coal bin was more efficient than the old way of having to constantly shovel coal directly into the furnace. That extra time saved was taken up by more mind-numbing, house labor.

I navigated through Naomi's house and the outside world wishing I was a ghost. I traveled with trepidation and avoided any eye contact. I approached blind corners carefully. I crossed from one side of the street to the other to avoid bullies. I stumbled through the stinking alleys in my old-man clown clothes. When I saw another human, I kept my eyes lowered, and hoped not to be noticed.

"It's the sissy."

"It's the freak."

"It's the retard."

"Watch the spastic stumble."

A punch to my eye brought stars and brilliantly-colored, streaky flashes to my vision.

A punch to my stomach brought pain and nausea.

A punch to my nose brought a spray of blood and overwhelming nausea.

A punch to my arm brought numbing pain and a lumpy bruise.

The worst was to see the spray of blood from my nose. I hated to feel my nose flatten against my face. I hated the blurry blaze of fireworks that flashed before my eyes.

At school, there was a boy who was half as tall as I was. The bullies called him midget, dwarf, runt, and pipsqueak. Here was someone I could pick on.

"Hey, midget," I taunted him.

He hit me in the face before I even had a thought to defend myself. He hit me again and again. His fists were boney and merciless. I staggered about in my oversized clothes and my clodhopper shoes.

"Let's watch the runt kick the retard's ass!" a gathering crowd of kids shouted.

I never called him a name after that, but he hit me plenty. He got into fights with anyone he could catch. If he couldn't catch the bullies who tormented him, he easily caught me and punched me. Being so short made him tough. Being picked on made him tough. He was lucky he wore clothes and shoes that fit him, and he was nimble. I always wore my ragged, oversized, old-man clothes. He became popular with the other kids by beating up on me. But he still had to endure being called a dwarf and a midget.

"Come on Shorty. Kick the freak's ass."

Chapter 18

The house next door to Naomi's sat on a double lot. That extra plot of land was owned and used by the neighbor for flower and vegetable gardens. An old mother and her middle-aged daughter lived in the two-story, brown-brick residence. The daughter had one leg in a brace and needed a crutch to walk. When she was in her garden working among her flowers and vegetables, she laid her crutch aside and balanced on her one good leg. She dragged her bad leg, with its heavy metal brace, behind her. Her useless limb hung at odd angles from her lower body and followed her everywhere.

"Her name is Margaret," Naomi had informed me. "She had polio. Don't bother her."

I watched Margaret work in her garden, and I wondered about her. Had she ever had a husband and children? I didn't think the answer was yes. She wasn't ugly like Naomi, but she never wore makeup or fashionable clothes or smiled like my mother had. She looked an unlikely candidate for romance and motherhood. I never saw any men visitors at her house. I didn't think there was any way a crippled person like her could run and play with children. That is if they didn't give their children away to strangers.

I liked to talk to her when Naomi wasn't watching me.

"My tulips are doing really well this year," she said.

"You sure know how to grow them, Margaret." Even though Margaret liked Naomi and I hated Naomi, I liked Margaret.

"You're really lucky Naomi gave you such a fine home, Mickey," Margaret said. "You should always be grateful to her. When she gets old, take care of her like she's your real mother. That's a child's duty."

"Yeah," I muttered. I guessed Margaret didn't see all the bad things Naomi did to me. Maybe she didn't see what Naomi did to me as being bad. Worse things could happen to me if I wasn't a slave to Naomi. Even though I walked oddly because of my oversized clodhopper shoes, I didn't need a crutch to get around. I was glad I didn't have to drag around a useless leg that had a heavy, steel brace on it.

"It's going to be an excellent garden this year," Margaret said as she uprooted a weed with her hoe.

"It sure looks great, Margaret."

I saw she loved to work in her garden and I suspected winter was tough on her.

A knocking against the glass of a partially open window on the first floor of Margaret's house interrupted us. I looked over and saw the outline of her old mother at the window.

"Margaret," a barely audible croak of a voice called out.

"I have to go in, Mickey," Margaret sighed as she laid her rake aside. "My mother needs me."

"Bye."

"See you tomorrow, Mickey." Margaret squeezed her crutch into her armpit and threw herself into motion. She moved rapidly towards the house. It always surprised me how swiftly she covered ground when she needed to.

"Margaret," her mother's tortured voice called out again.

"I'm coming, mother. I'm coming."

Another friend of mine, besides Margaret, was the ragman. I met him during my walks to and from school, the only freedom the beast Naomi allowed me away from my labors and my isolation in my room. An elderly, colored person, he owned an equally old, dirty-gray, swaybacked horse that pulled his wagon loaded with rags through the alley behind Naomi's house. He called out at the top of his deep, voice.

"Rag man! The rag man's here!"

The first time I met Otis, he worried me. He was so black and wrinkled. He had large, big-knuckled hands and a stern look on his pitted face. He grumbled at me, but he let me pet his horse that was as bony, scarred and ugly as he was.

It was a challenge to find a place on the horse I wanted to touch, let alone pet.

"This horse is pretty old, isn't he, sir?"

"You is a raggedy, little white boy," he frowned at me.

"Yes sir, I know I am." I believed Otis thought I was criticizing his horse.

"Still, you are white." His frightening frown changed to a trace of a smile. "You are so white, boy."

Still unsure, I forced a small smile back at him.

"Raggedy," he repeated, but now with a trace of sympathy in his voice. "Though, it's better being a raggedy little white boy, than any sort of black boy."

I saw only a few yellow, crooked teeth in his whole mouth. "Yes sir, I guess it is."

I thought anything was better than being me. I'd like to be Otis. I'd like to own a horse and a wagon. I'd like to be grown up and strong. The best part about Otis was that he was free. I really envied his freedom. I didn't want his rotten teeth and wrinkly skin though.

"What's your horse's name, sir?"

"His name is Horse."

Horse swished his scraggly tail and blinked his drippy eyes to chase away the flies that constantly attacked him.

I didn't know much about coloreds and wasn't sure what they were interested in talking about. "Were you a slave?" I asked.

Otis's smile disappeared. A deep scowl took over his face. I couldn't figure out what had changed. His look of anger scared me. I didn't need more people looking at me like I was some kind of dirty vermin.

"You think I was a slave?" he growled at me.

"I didn't mean anything, sir," I stammered. "It's just I heard and seen things about coloreds being slaves. We studied a little bit about slavery in school."

"I'm a slave to this horse. I'm a slave to this wagon full of rags. I'm a slave to earning enough money to have a place to sleep and buy food to feed me and this old nag."

He moved his face forward, so his glare was closer to me.

"I'm sorry, sir." Jesus. I wouldn't ever say slave to a colored person again.

"You're too young to understand much, boy." Otis looked down at his gnarly, big-veined hands. He clenched the reins so tightly, those veins stood up even more, and I worried they'd pop open, and Otis would bleed to death. I edged away from him and his wagon. I was ready to move on, but Otis was a valuable friend, and I didn't want him to stay mad at me.

"I didn't know, sir. I'm sorry."

"It's okay. I'm not angry with you, boy. You need to understand because someone is old and black doesn't mean they was a slave."

"Yes, sir."

"Got to get back to work," Otis sighed. He snapped the reins over Horse's back. "Move on, Horse."

Horse had fallen asleep. His head jerked up, and he blinked his eyes. His body surged forward a few inches and caught the weight of the wagon. He strained against the load. The wagon creaked. Horse wheezed. Otis snapped the reins harder against Horse's bony back and yelled. "Move on, Horse."

I watched them as they rattled down the alley.

Otis shouted, "Rag man! The rag man is here."

I was glad Otis wasn't totally mad at me. I wanted to visit him and

Horse again. A raggedy kid like me never knew when and where he'd find a friend.

Damn. I really wished I owned a horse and a wagon. I really wished I was free from the monster Naomi.

Over time, Otis told me some of his family history.

"So, you won't be so ignorant, boy," he said.

It was difficult to understand everything he said, but gradually, I straightened his words out in my mind.

Otis rambled on, "My mother told me stories about my grandmother. My grandmother had been a slave. She was betrayed and sold by her own family in Africa because she was a girl and a burden to her parents and they didn't want to own her anymore.

"A slave trader bought her cheap. She survived a long land trip across Africa to a slave-ship port. She said she saw many people die on the land crossing. Terrible things happened that a boy as young as you doesn't need to hear about. She survived the wretched trip from the coast of Africa to America in a rotten old ship. Lots of those Africans on that filthy vessel died during the crossing. Their bodies were tossed into the ocean for the sharks to eat.

"After that death ship arrived in America, my grandmother was sold at a slave auction in South Carolina. They forced her to be a field slave. She worked long hours under the blazing, hot sun picking cotton. Then, there was the bloody Civil War, and Abraham Lincoln freed the slaves. My grandmother traveled north where she got married and worked as a house servant. My grandfather was killed in an accident while he was digging a tunnel for the city. But my mother was born a free woman."

During the telling of Otis's story, Horse had fallen asleep. A nearby fight between two alley cats upset a garbage can lid. The lid clanged to the ground and Horse was startled awake.

"Goddamn alley cats," I said. "I hate them."

"Don't use the Lord's name like that."

"Sorry."

"Anyway," Otis said. "I wasn't born no gosh darn slave."

Otis and I laughed.

"Yes sir," I said.

I liked Otis, and I hoped he and I'd stay friends forever.

I didn't tell him anything about Naomi and how she beat me. I didn't tell him about my mother giving me away. I didn't want him to know I was a kid nobody wanted. I didn't want him to know the awful stuff that made me look like a weak sissy. I wanted Otis to think I was much stronger and braver than I really was.

"I wish I had better clothes," I said. "I wish I had clothes that fit me."

"Yeah, you could use some better clothes," he said. "I've seen worse, though. Still, you got blond hair, and you got blue eyes. Believe me, boy, being so white will help you a lot."

"You think so, sir?"

"It sure will, boy."

So far, my blond hair and blue eyes hadn't made life easier for me. I suspected Naomi hated me even more because of the way I looked. My father certainly hated me for the way I looked. He'd always called me "Blondie" in a cruel, degrading way. Otis didn't know my truth. Nobody did except me. It wasn't a truth I wanted to share.

The alleys were home to a different flow of life. At times, those narrow passageways were much friendlier and safer than Chicago's wide, traffic-clogged streets. The alleys were sort of a refuge for me, except when it was really hot, and the stink drove me away. In the summer, overflowing garbage baked in the sun. There were dead rats and dead cats and dog shit and horseshit and flies and maggots and sometimes I thought there had to be dying or dead people amongst all the garbage.

People like Otis lived off the alleys. I hoped his house didn't smell like this place where he spent so much of his life.

"I never had a wife or a family or a nice farm to live on," Otis had declared in a voice tinged with sadness. "My life never worked out that way."

A junk man, who also owned a horse-drawn wagon, sifted through the trash and garbage looking for people's throwaways he could salvage and sell.

"Junk man! It's the junk man here!" he called out in his thick accent. He wanted his presence known, in case people who were within range of his voice had junk they wanted to get rid of, but they had forgotten to put the stuff out with the garbage.

A friendly older man, he said he was born in Italy. Naples, Italy.

"My name is Romano."

"I'm Mickey, sir," I had to keep reminding him.

Romano had a swarthy, wide face with huge eyebrows that nearly hid his small eyes. A dense beard and mustache, a bulbous, red nose and thin lips over uneven, yellow teeth completed his ugly face. He chewed tobacco, which dribbled down onto his mustache and beard. He constantly turned his head sideways to spit. He and his clothes were covered with a thick layer of dirt and dust, and his wagon overflowed with a clutter of every throwaway imaginable. How Romano saw a use for his collection of worn out, broken objects mystified me. The best items he kept close to him under his seat on the floorboard of his wagon.

As sorry as Otis's horse looked, Romano's horse looked even worse. The poor creature was a dirty, faded-brown color, with insect tortured sores, ragged scars, and patches of hide missing. His bones were prominent everywhere on his body, and his hoofs were chipped and cracked. Flies constantly tortured his drippy, sad eyes. Still, I guessed he was better off than the poor horses I'd seen herded into Chicago's slaughterhouses to be hit over the head with a sledgehammer, gutted, and chopped up into dog food.

"There's a difference between junk and garbage," Romano said. "Some people's junk is my treasure. Garbage is garbage, and I don't want any of that."

"Yes, sir. You've got some great looking stuff there."

"Real treasures they are," Romano beamed. "I know exactly what to pick. I fix it so it's like new and I sell all of it."

He flipped the reins along the deeply swayed back of his horse. Struggling mightily, the old nag got the wagon moving.

"Junk man here! I'm the junk man!" His voice sang out loudly.

The junk man, Romano, was entertaining, but he wasn't a close friend like Otis.

Across the street from Ryerson School, a small, older woman named Bunny lived in a basement apartment and used her small front room as a store. I walked the six steps down from the sidewalk, and if the sign on her door said "Open," I walked in. A bell, operated by a string contraption, rang when the door opened, and Bunny would appear through the curtained doorway that led to her kitchen, bedroom, and bathroom. A glass counter like the candy counters in movie theatres took up most of her front room. The glass top and the two shelves below it were crowded with candies and school supplies.

Bunny served a rush of business before school, during lunch, and after school. She didn't have a loud voice, but she demanded that the children behave while in her store and they listened or were told to leave. If I'd dared to steal a few coins from Naomi's change purse, which the monster kept on the top of her dresser, and Bunny's place wasn't too busy, I bought candy. I needed to time my movements to avoid the bullies, and I needed to be sure I arrived home before Naomi decided I was late and punished me with her screeching curses and brutal fists. Bunny acted like she understood my difficulties when she greeted me warmly. Her friendliness both comforted and frightened me. I mistrusted and was wary of most humans.

There weren't any clues in Bunny's basement apartment that a husband or any children existed in her life. It appeared she lived alone and operated her small store because she liked the children. I knew some people liked children and many others hated them. Too often, kids misbehave. My own mother didn't want the burden of her rowdy sons. I waited and waited, but Mom didn't come back to rescue me from Naomi. I feared she really didn't want me to ever be her kid anymore.

Chapter 19

"It's been over a year since your mother dumped you here, so you must be ten-years-old," Naomi growled. "But why should I care. She certainly doesn't care what became of you."

My birthday was actually a few months ago. I was ten-years-old when I became asthmatic. I didn't believe I'd ever breathe easily again. Maybe it was from the coal dust in the basement. Maybe it was because of the worn-thin, raggedy old-man clothes the monster forced me to wear during the cold, wet days. Maybe it was punishment God cursed me with because I hated Naomi so much. It was even more difficult to breathe when Naomi screamed and beat me. I was slowed down by hacking coughs and bronchial rattles. Constant croaks, whistles, wheezes, and sneezes plagued me. I was a symphony of noises. A waterfall of snot escaped my nose. Where the hell does all that snot come from?

Every known and unknown childhood illness invaded my scrawny body.

"You're useless!" Naomi's anger grew with each of my new maladies. "I didn't take you into my house to nurse you. You're supposed to be working."

Fevers and chills coursed through me. A rash that never stopped itching covered my body. Forces which were as evil as Naomi attacked me from inside my body.

"You have to get back to work!" she screamed. "I don't care how sick you are."

Mumps, chickenpox and scarlet fever found a welcoming entry into my weakened system.

Vomiting and diarrhea kept me on the run. I spent more and more time hanging my head over or sitting on the toilet.

When I grew too weak to climb up the stairway to my second-floor room, a cot in the narrow hallway next to the bathroom became my home.

Naomi buried me under layers of blankets. "You need to sweat it out."

I sweated.

I moaned.

I vomited.

I suffered terrifying dreams. Gigantic reptilian creatures chased me down and swallowed me whole. I suffocated in the stinking seas of bile that filled their huge stomachs. Other times I fell into blazing pits of fire, and my skin bubbled up into huge blisters, or I flailed hopelessly in stormy, icy oceans and sank under the merciless waters and drowned.

Naomi forced me to drink putrid brews. She rubbed foul-scented concoctions on my bony chest with her rough and angry hands.

Her hate for me blazed to a new brilliance. "You're useless. I should throw you out into the street."

My throat swelled to where I couldn't swallow. I felt too weak to care what the monster did to me anymore. I knew I was dying and welcomed my end.

"I don't have time to nurse you!" She raged.

I spent days, then weeks in delirium. My ever-ghastlier nightmares were a preview of the hell I read about in the Bible, and Naomi always said I was destined for. A gleeful Satan stabbed me with his red-hot pitchfork and hell's blazing flames consumed me. I sweated gallons of saltwater that soaked my sheets. My lips parched drier than the most brutal desert ever trod by man.

She piled on more blankets.

I puked.

"Clean up your mess, you pig."

I shit.

"You are such a worthless bastard."

All the sins I'd committed throughout my childhood made the inferno I staggered through my just punishment. My constant hoping for Naomi to die was my worst transgression witnessed daily by God.

But I survived.

"Now, get back to work, stupid!" the monster bellowed.

It was time again for me to make a grocery-shopping trip.

Every muscle in my body tensed and it got difficult to breathe. I wanted to flee to the world's densest, darkest forest and hide there forever.

"Here's the list," Naomi said. "There are five items at the bottom I want you to sneak into your pockets. I'm giving you enough money to pay for everything except those five items."

"I'm afraid to do that," I protested. "What if they catch me?"

"If you're careful, you won't get caught!" she yelled. "I'm telling you to do it."

"I'm afraid."

She grabbed me by my hair. She twisted with all her brutish strength. The pain was excruciating. "You'd better be afraid of me!" She slapped me violently on my ear with the flat of her hand. The terrible ringing noise returned and reverberated throughout my head.

"I'm sorry," I pleaded. "I'll do it."

She let go of my hair. I backed away from her. I cupped my hand over my throbbing ear. My scalp stung like it had been stuck with a million, red-hot needles.

As I walked the four blocks to the grocery store, I kept a sharp lookout for the neighborhood bullies.

I pushed the shopping cart up and down the narrow aisles of the store. I held the shopping list in my hand. I read the list again and again. I'd picked out all the items the beast had given me money to pay for. I walked by the tins of pepper and cinnamon Naomi had ordered me to slip into the deep pockets of my oversized, old-man trousers, and the two cans of sardines, and on another aisle, I walked by the blue Rit dye she'd ordered me to steal. I walked another aisle, and I glanced around to see if anyone watched me. I turned into another aisle. I worried about the sudden appearance of a copper who'd grab me by my collar and haul me away and throw me into a watery prison dungeon that was home to hungry, razor-toothed rats. Like submarines cruising on the surface of the seas, the rats would swim directly towards my face and clamp their filthy teeth deep into my nose. To be arrested as a thief and beaten with thick, wooden clubs by raging prison guards scared the hell out of me, but Naomi's violent punishment scared me even more.

I'd already taken more time for this shopping trip than I was supposed to, and the monster would beat me for that anyway, so I gave up on my thievery mission.

"Why didn't you do as I told you?" Naomi screamed. She grabbed my hair and twisted with all her strength. She swung me back and forth like a rag doll. She slapped my cheek. Hard. "You're going back tomorrow. You'd better come home with those items in your pockets!"

She finally released my hair. I fell to the floor. My face and scalp face throbbed from the pain inflicted by the brute's murderous hands. I wished I'd die. I never want to look in the beast's hate-filled eyes again. I wanted to kill her so bad I could barely breathe.

The clerks at the market were suspicious of me from the moment I entered their store and stood guard at the end of each aisle I shopped in. They reminded me of twitchy-tailed, alley cats stalking a filthy rat as it gobbled down a morsel of garbage. I bowed my head and scurried from aisle to aisle, but I couldn't get out of their sight.

I was unsuccessful again. Resigned to the pain of my awaiting punishment, I returned to Naomi.

"They were watching me all the time." I cowered and cringed as I begged for mercy.

Enraged, she cursed me, she grabbed me by my hair, and she twisted me to the floor and hit me across my back and my shoulders with her broomstick.

"Damn you. You're going to a different store," she yelled. "You owe me lots of money for keeping you fed and housed. Goddamn, you and your rotten, whore of a mother."

Finally, I resigned myself to being her thief and developed a superior stealing skill. I got better at thievery than when I was eight-years-old and stole candy bars from old Jew shopkeepers with my two older brothers. I struggled to remember the wonderful time when I lived with my mother and Mom still loved me, and she still hugged me.

Chapter 20

Once a month, Naomi sent me downtown by bus to buy a Swedish language newspaper for Emil. The bus turnaround and boarding place were a few blocks from the house. The bus trip might have been a fun escape from my painful daily routine, except Naomi ordered me to lie to the driver about my age so I could get the little child's free fare. Obviously, I wasn't a five-year-old kid as she ordered me to claim. I dreaded the monthly charade. I argued with the same drivers over and over. The looks they gave me as I approached and boarded their bus made me feel like a cheating criminal. Naomi gave me the exact amount of money for the cost of the newspaper, and if I returned to her without Emil's Swedish newspaper, I knew she'd explode into a rage and beat me.

I approached the bus and saw that it was the meanest driver.

"So, it's you again kid."

"Yes, sir."

"You're not going to lie to me about your age today, are you kid?"

"No, sir."

"Put your nickel into the fare box then."

"I'm only five-years-old, sir. I'm almost six, but I'm still five, sir."

"You're lying to me again, kid."

"I'm only five-years-old, sir."

"That's a damn lie. You've got to be eight-years-old, and you owe the kid's fare."

"I'm only five, sir."

"Damn. Go ahead and get aboard kid, but don't pull this trick again."

"Thank you, sir."

After enduring an hour of jerky stops and starts aboard the bus and feeling sick from the motion and from breathing diesel fumes, I exited on State Street. I bought the Swedish language newspaper at a stand that carried newspapers and magazines from all over the world. I waited for the same bus making its return trip to Garfield Park. My short wait at State Street was the highlight of the trip. I liked to look at the covers of the magazines decorated with pictures of pretty, young women and cliff-side towns close to the sea. I could become a sailor someday and travel to these wonderful places.

The return-to-Naomi bus pulled up at the stop. I climbed up the steps. I argued with the driver about the fare. I endured another nausea-inducing, hour-long bus ride as a lowdown liar and conniving cheat.

Another huge pain involved with my monthly trips was the bus ride took me through some of my old neighborhoods and hangouts. I revisited areas of Chicago where my brothers and I'd experienced wonderful adventures. I always looked carefully for a sighting of them or Mom.

Through the bus window, I spotted a trim and neatly dressed woman who wore high heels and walked intently along the crowded downtown sidewalk. The glamorous woman puffed deeply on a cigarette. I was sure it was Mom.

"Mom," I shouted. I banged my hand on the bus window. "Mom, it's me. It's your son Mickey!"

People outside on the sidewalk and people inside the bus turned and stared at me.

"Mom," I called louder.

"What's going on back there?" the bus driver yelled.

As we passed the walking woman, I saw it wasn't Mom. I crunched down as low as I could in my seat and hid my face. Damn. She'd looked like Mom from the back. I'd felt so elated for a few seconds.

Two tough-looking boys strode along the sidewalk with an air of confidence and cockiness. I was sure it was Tommy and Ben. I banged on the bus window with the flat of my hand.

"Tommy! Ben! It's me. It's your brother Mickey!"

"Stop that yelling, kid," A cranky woman across the aisle yelled at me.

I jumped up and ran down the center aisle of the bus to the middle exit door. I pulled the cord that signaled the driver I wanted to disembark. I pushed against the exit door with both hands.

"Please stop, driver. Let me off the bus. Those are my two older brothers."

More frantic now, I pushed against the door with my shoulder. The two boys saw me. They pointed at me and laughed. They both mouthed the word "Stupid" at me. Damn. It wasn't Tommy and Ben.

The driver glanced back at me over his shoulder and yelled, "Stop that racket kid, or I'll get the police after you."

I went back to my seat. I wanted to disappear. I heard an old woman's voice say, "That little boy is crazy."

The hell with what people thought of me. I wouldn't ever quit looking for Mom and my brothers. I wouldn't ever quit hoping they'd see me, recognize me, and we'd be back together as a happy family.

"Hey, there's Mickey!" I imagined Mom and Tommy and Ben's voices. We'd gather together and hug each other as tightly as we could. We'd all shed tears. I'd be saved from my ordeal of living with the monster, Naomi.

Whenever I boarded a bus and walked down the center aisle, I glanced at every face I passed. I hoped for a familiar and friendly response. But mostly I saw indifference. When seated, I closely observed each new passenger who boarded the bus. Many times, I thought I saw Mom or Tommy or Ben. It always turned out to be a stranger.

Too many times I looked into the wanting eyes of one of those men who were on the prowl for lonely, young boys. Then, I shrunk down inside myself and avoided all eye contact as I waited for the predator to leave the bus.

Often, I sat right behind the driver hoping for protection from both the predators and the bullies who enjoyed picking on weak-looking kids. Whether I sat on a bus, walked to school, or stood in a crowd of people, I tried to position myself for escape. A kid like me always had to be careful.

Alone in my room and out of tears, I grasped my face in my hands and pressed my fingertips into my flesh. I tried to pull out the ugliness that tortured my mind. But I couldn't pull the ugliness out. The ugliness kept growing inside of me. I forced a grimace onto my face to distort my features, but I couldn't stay as ugly on the outside as I felt inside. I screamed silently until my throat hurt. I squeezed my eyes tighter and tighter as I looked for blackness, but fireworks kept the light on. I tensed all my muscles and screamed silently again and again until I thought my head would explode into a thousand bloody fragments. I tried to die by not breathing, but I wasn't strong and brave enough to hold my breath until I died.

I tried to remember the sight and sound of my mother and brothers, but they'd grown dimmer and dimmer in my memory. I didn't have physical contact from any human being except beatings from Naomi, and beatings from the bullies on the street and at school.

I lay on the floor next to the door that separated my room from the renters'. I pressed my ear up to the narrow space between the door and the floor. I listened to their television's nonstop and fascinating sounds, blended with the renter's voices and laughter. The couple commented about the scenes on television. They saw comical images. They listened to hilarious words. I created pictures in my mind to match all the words and sounds I heard coming from under the door. I loved television.

A younger couple, I guessed was their son and daughter-in-law, visited them often.

"What's happening with the kid who lives with your landlord?" the son asked.

"I believe he's either doing work for Naomi, or he's alone in his room. I've never seen him out playing or have other kids over to visit and play."

"Is he in there now?" asked the daughter-in-law.

"I'm sure he is."

"He stays really quiet most of the time."

"I think he listens to us."

"Isn't that creepy?"

"He's just a little boy."

"I think his mother left him with Naomi and disappeared. I 've never seen her visit him. What an awful thing to do to your own child."

"Naomi isn't a pleasant woman."

"She scares me!"

Laughter

"At least she doesn't smoke. And, I've never seen her drunk. Emil doesn't appear to have any bad habits either."

"He does have poor taste in women."

There was more laughter.

"I've never seen anyone visit the kid."

"Isn't there something going on here that's against the law?"

"I don't think so."

"His mother just left him here one day. Who knows what the story is on his father."

"There isn't anything we can do."

"If we stick our nose in, we could lose this apartment."

"I feel so sorry for him though. I hear him crying. He's in there all by himself, and he cries."

"He won't talk to us when we see him."

"He won't look at us either."

"Maybe he's retarded."

I quietly retreated from the door. Damn. I wished the young couple would take me home with them. She sounded gentle, and he didn't sound like he'd want to beat up a kid. I bet they ate delicious food all the time and lots of it. But there wasn't any way they'd want to own something like me.

I crawled into my bed and pulled the covers over my head. I needed to hide in the dark. I couldn't listen to those voices anymore. Their words made me appear to be a worse freak than I already was. I burrowed deep into the blackness under the covers. Everyone thought I was a retard. I tensed my body until I was as stiff as a slab of concrete and I couldn't feel anything. I imagined I was an Egyptian King who'd become a mummy. I was buried in a casket ornamented with layers of gold and studded with hundreds of huge jewels. Throughout the country, thousands of people gathered and sobbed and wailed because I died.

I couldn't maintain my rigid posture. Exhausted by my effort, I relaxed my aching body.

What's going to happen to me?

When Naomi exploded in rage and screamed at me and beat me, she often grew short of breath and had to stop beating me, so she could sit down and rest. She turned pale, and sweat appeared on her brow. Her body expanded and contracted like the bellows Emil used to flame up the fire in the fireplace. She gasped for air. At those moments, I thought she might fall over dead. But no, she always recovered.

I remembered cartoons I'd seen with my brothers at the movie matinees a long time ago. If I was quick enough and brave enough to run dizzying circles around Naomi, she'd become crazy with rage because she couldn't grab me. Screaming at the top of her lungs, she'd grow overheated and explode into a million globs of bloody flesh.

A paralyzing fear gripped me. What if Naomi never died? I wouldn't ever leave this room and go outside to play. I'd be isolated in this tiny space forever, and Naomi would beat me forever. I'd be her house-slave forever. I'd always be Naomi's sneaky shoplifter and dress like a freak for the rest of my life.

What would happen to me if I got old, like twelve or thirteen? If Naomi didn't kill me before then, I might be able to kill her. Would the law be on her side? I could tell the coppers she beat me. Was there a law against beating kids? There probably wasn't. Most people beat their kids. Was there a law that said kids were supposed to be allowed to go outside and play? Mom had quit school and gone to work in a factory when she was fourteen-years-old. I'm only ten.

Naomi might just throw me out in the street like she always threatened. She could get a new kid that was smaller and weaker like I was when Mom left me here over a year ago. Of course, I might always be weak and scared, no matter how big I grew.

If Naomi did kill me, she could stuff my body into her furnace. The fire in the furnace got hot enough to burn anything to ashes. She could mix my ashes with the coal ashes, and no one would ever know what happened to me. If somebody asked about me, she could lie and say I ran away. People always believed the grownups, not the kids. No one would ever know and care what became of me. No one cared now. I'd simply disappear.

Did Mom ever think about me? Did she ever wonder what I was doing? Did she remember me as a baby? I'm sure she loved me then. I remembered her holding me. She told me she called me "Pretty Mickey" when I was a baby. But I got older and did bad things. Was I so awful that no parents would ever have wanted to keep me?

I dreamed about Mom. I still wanted her to come back to rescue me. No matter how hard I tried not to, I still loved her.

Chapter 21

I continued to read the Holy Bible. I finished Genesis and started reading Exodus.

And Moses stretched out his hand over the sea; and the Lord caused the sea to go back by a strong east wind all that night, and made the sea dry land, and the waters were divided.

And the children of Israel went into the midst of the sea upon the dry ground: and the waters were a wall unto them on their right hand, and on their left.

Exodus 14: 21 & 22

What a great man Moses was. I didn't want to imagine walking between two high walls of water, though. It was too much like the abyss of my nightmares.

I continued my struggle reading Pilgrim's Progress.

Now, Faithful, play the man, speak for thy God;
Fear not the wicked's malice, nor their rod:
Speak boldly, man, the truth is on thy side:
Die for it, and to Life in triumph ride.

Speak boldly. I didn't think so. Not unless you wanted to get beat up more. I knew I wasn't brave enough to speak up and endure more beatings. I wanted to avoid beatings, not ask for more. I didn't understand how dying would be a victory over my enemies. I wanted to see all my enemies suffer and die.

I often prayed Naomi might magically transform into a gentle person and not treat me so badly. While I labored on my hands and knees, she sat in her favorite chair and read her bible. I hoped she'd read the words about goodness and decide to follow those lessons from the Holy Scriptures. The bible also said sparing the rod would spoil the child. I guessed those were Naomi's favorite words in the Holy Book. Naomi was good at using the rod as the bible told her to. And, there was also the guy in the bible that was ready to kill his own son to please God. Maybe, Naomi thought beating a boy like me to death would make God happy, and he'd welcome her into heaven.

I prayed Naomi would just ignore me sometimes like her mind was totally confused, and she'd forgotten I existed. My prayers to God for help, which I repeated nightly, didn't appear to be working.

Moving on to the next grade in school gave me a kinder teacher. Reading the Bible and Pilgrims Progress had made me a much better reader than any of the other kids in my grade. On a reading test at school, I scored so well the teacher had me read aloud in my classroom and in a higher-grade classroom. The positive teacher told me I was so good at reading, I should become a doctor, a lawyer or a college professor. Or even a writer. I liked that teacher, but I didn't like the attention she showered on me. I wanted to be like the other children, not the "teacher's pet." Kids chanted those words at me now. I guess I wasn't a mental retard. I was just a physical retard, spastic and freak.

From my window, I saw many birds. I loved to watch their activities.

Doves, in pairs, sat on nearby power lines and cooed. They never left their mate alone and abandoned.

Fearless woodpeckers climbed, clung to and tapped a nearby tree trunk. The tree branches spread wide, and the longest branch scratched against my window.

Sparrows searched for seeds on the small area of roof my window overlooked. They hopped about as if on pogo sticks.

Red-breasted robins gathered on the grassy lawn below and captured worms in their beaks. They stretched those pale brown bodies to transparency.

Several noisy black crows boldly swooped downward to the pavement of Hamlin Avenue and hurriedly feasted on traffic-flattened squirrels. Yuck.

I watched the bird's antics and wished I could escape from Naomi and join them. I would live with them forever.

One painfully-lonely day, as I lay on my bed, a black-masked redbird landed on my windowsill. He looked at me through the glass. I stayed as still as a corpse in a casket. That bird tilted his bright-red head and stared at me with increasing curiosity. He whistled at me like he meant to say words of comfort. I marveled at his friendly courage. I wanted to reach out and touch redbird. I wanted to show him a boy like me could be gentle.

I wished redbird would stay at my window forever. I didn't want to be alone anymore.

Too soon, after one last whistle, my redbird friend flew away. Redbird hadn't intended to tease and torture me. His presence made me feel I was a part of his world. His absence left me feeling abandoned.

When I ran the streets of Chicago with my older brothers, we threw rocks at birds. Now, birds eased the pain of my forced solitude. My sealed-shut window muted their chatter, but during moments free of traffic noise, the birds sang melodies to me. It was the sweetest music I ever heard.

Those fancy fliers moved freely in the world. Birds reminded me of possibility. In my happy thoughts, I soared up into the sky alongside my feathered friends.

Naomi played cards with women close to her in age and older, and of equal social standing. These well-dressed, old women sat four to a table as they played and gossiped non-stop. Refreshments were served when they took a break from their game. Dressed in my raggedy, oversized, old-man clothes, I sat on a chair against the wall and waited for the serving of the treats these women had prepared. My stomach rumbled in anticipation of sweetened coffee or tea, and the delicious assortment of cookies and cakes.

"What a handsome boy you are," a hunchbacked, white-haired, old woman said, as she

walked by me. Her trembling, claw-shaped hand gripped her cane.

Naomi sat at a table not far away, ignoring me.

"Naomi," her card partner said, "You are so generous to have taken that poor little boy into your home. How could a mother abandon a child like that?"

"I like to do what's right," Naomi bragged.

"The Lord will bless you, Naomi," the woman said. She turned and looked at me with a warm, loving smile.

"Yes. God will bless you, Naomi," another old, creaking voice agreed.

These women gazed upon me with affection. I felt their desire to pet me as if I was a furry, little dog. Most of the women appeared kind. But, the thought of being touched in any way filled me with dread. But I did look forward to the sweets they lovingly baked.

My life might be so much better living with anybody in this room besides Naomi. Maybe, it'd be better. People could fool you. These women liked Naomi. At home, were they just like her? I couldn't believe they were. I didn't sense brutal meanness radiate from any of them. Still, a kid never knew for sure which adult would turn out to be cruel.

Most of the women wore thick makeup, pricey clothes and lots of jewelry. The fine clothes draped loosely on hunched-over, bony old frames. The large-bodied women needed yards of expensive material to cover their girth. Strings of pearls and gold necklaces hung around fleshy, wrinkled necks. Fleshy arms that sagged and jiggled ended in fat wrists adorned with gold bracelets and delicate, jeweled watches. Hands with prominent purple veins had big-knuckled fingers weighed down with gold and silver rings imbedded with sparkling diamonds and multicolored, precious stones.

It appeared to me the big, red and blue veins that popped out from these old women's bodies were ready to burst and flood the room in blood. I'd be drowned by a crimson tidal wave.

I waited and watched as the women played their card game. Cackling laughter caused the creases in their faces to multiply and grow deeper.

Naomi dressed up for these gatherings. She wore a black dress that matched the finery of her friends. She adorned herself with a pearl necklace, a jeweled gold bracelet and the large, diamond wedding ring that cut into the flesh of my face when she hit me. She had scrubbed that ring clean of my blood, and it sparkled. She layered makeup on her face to hide her oldness and ugliness. Her rare smile was forced and phony. Yet these people couldn't see through her mask or sense her brutal meanness.

I was the only male at these gatherings. Some talk at the tables was about husbands long dead. A couple of fragile, old men dressed in black suits with white shirts and dark ties, smiled and bowed when they showed up at the end of the festivities to escort their wives home. They ignored my presence.

Like most of her old, woman friends, Naomi colored her hair to hide its dingy-gray roots. She made me steal the packages of hair coloring and forced me to apply those stinking chemicals to the dingy-gray roots that sprouted from her scaly scalp.

I brushed the brown color onto her hair roots, a handful at a time.

"Be careful you idiot! That stung." She swung her elbow angrily into my ribs. The impact made me gasp for breath. I hurriedly continued one of my most dreaded and disgusting jobs.

The beast let me wear heavily stained, rubber gloves to protect my hands, but the noxious fumes from the chemicals constantly punished my nose and eyes. I hated the beast's stinky body-odor, foul breath and constant harping and was repulsed by this forced, intimate contact. But she didn't give me any choice.

Chapter 22

The best part of working for hours in the basement was escape from Naomi.

The unfinished underside of the wood floor in Naomi's apartment showed above heavy support beams. The oak floor she carelessly plodded across glowed because of the hours I spent on hands and knees waxing and shining. I hate the smell of paste wax.

I used a broom to sweep away the spider webs in the spaces between the wood beams. Globs of spider web fell onto my face and shoulders. I prayed that no live, black-widow spiders landed on me and crawled down my shirt.

As Naomi lumbered through her apartment, the floorboards creaked and groaned. If I had magical powers, I would reach through the thick wood flooring with the broom and trip the cruel cow. She'd fall over like a giant tree, land flat on her face, and break every bone in her ugly mug. She would die, and nobody would ever know I killed her.

The windows of the basement were too stained by coal dust to let in much light, and Naomi used the cheapest, dimmest light bulbs down there. I felt imprisoned in a subterranean dungeon. I tried to avoid the darkest, scariest recesses of the basement, but my work forced me into those terrifying places. The hair rose on my scalp as I imagined the rotted corpse of one of Naomi's former child slaves coming back to life and seeking revenge.

As I crept about the basement, I heard scratching noises and saw flashes of movement.

RATS!

I was driven to the edge of hysterical flight.

Naomi forced me to set rat traps and place them in the darkest recesses of the basement. Those killing contraptions were the largest size available with tremendous spring power. I baited them with bloody chunks of liver or rotten smelling cheese. My hands trembled as I struggled to pull back the killing edge and set the locking bar. Sprung traps flew through the air if I panicked and released the bow.

When I put my hand and most of my arm into the dark places where the rats and their litters of blind babies lived, I visualized the mother rat attacking me leaving only a bloody stub at the end of my arm, or me accidentally setting off a trap and amputating my own fingers.

Even worse than setting them was the horror of retrieving the sprung traps and removing the dead rat bodies. At least, I hoped the trap held a dead body. If the rat was caught by its tail or part of a leg, it could gnaw itself free and leave its bloody body-part behind in the trap. When it was caught, but not dead, it would flop around as I reached in with a rake to pull it out of the dark hole and kill it myself.

Goddamn.

Jesus Christ.

Manny and Max sniffed and growled at the rat bodies I shook loose from the bloodstained traps and dropped on the concrete floor. If they didn't spring back to life and fight the dogs, I scooped up the dead bodies with a shovel, tossed them into the furnace, and watched them burn to a crisp in the red-hot flames.

I heard Naomi approach and make her awkward climb down the narrow stairway. The monster panted for breath as her heavy bulk reached the bottom of the stairs. Her blazing eyes spotted me, and she closed in to trap me in a corner.

"You made me climb down those stairs, you idiot! When will you ever learn? How can anyone be so stupid?"

I knew what was coming and cringed. She hit me across my back with the broom handle she clutched in her hand.

The impact of the stiff, wooden-rod stung, but I didn't cry out.

"You fat cow," I raged inside. "I hate you so much."

Thoughts only! Believe me, those were my thoughts only. I wasn't idiot enough to say those words out loud to her. I didn't want to die by her hand. I didn't want to give her the satisfaction of killing me.

"What are you up to, you monster?" she screamed.

Jesus Christ! She didn't remember or care why she was mad at me. She didn't really need a reason to rage at me. I'm sure she stored up hundreds of my faults in her mind, so she was always ready to explode in fury and attack me.

Most times, if Naomi had company during my working hours, I stayed in the basement. As I labored, I listened to the muffled voices and muted footsteps above me. She and her visitors drank tea with cream and lumps of sugar and nibbled on delicious fruit-filled pastries.

I stole sugar lumps when I worked in the kitchen. I stole anything I could eat, but I had to be quick. I grabbed wayward morsels, stuffed them in my mouth and kept my head bowed low so my chewing and swallowing couldn't be detected by the devil. Often, I swallowed without chewing. Pieces of raw dough, bits of food stuck to baking pans, stems, roots and peelings from fruit and vegetables were all edible. My kitchen work gave me opportunities for tiny bites of food. Cooked or uncooked, taste didn't matter.

Day by day, I was turning into a super-silent sneak and a masterful thief.

Chapter 23

Chicago's brutal winter loomed close. When the coal room was nearly empty, a truck loaded with canvas bags full of coal chunks arrived in front of the house and parked at the curb. A short, muscular man slung two fifty-pound bags of shiny-black coal over his back. He hurried at a pace close to a run to traverse the forty feet from the street and up the walkway alongside the house. He dumped the bags of coal through a ground-level, half-window that accessed the coal room.

After numerous trips, black chunks were piled up to the windowsill of the coal room. He shuffled into the basement and shoveled the coal to the back of the coal room and returned to carrying bags of coal. I never saw him stand up straight, so I guessed his back was permanently bent like a hunchback. I didn't know if God created him that way or if his deformed back was caused by his merciless occupation. He labored until the coal room was full before he paused to rest.

When he finally stopped, the muscles of his body kept vibrating. It didn't seem as if his body would ever relax. He started out as a white man, but now his broad face and large hands were black from coal dust, only the whites and the brown centers of his bloodshot eyes stood out. Coal dust coated his sweat-drenched clothes. I handed him a glass of water, and he smiled at me, even his teeth and tongue were stained with coal dust. He spoke with a thick foreign accent, and I didn't understand his words, but his courtesy and appreciation were obvious. His body was a mass of tight muscle, but his face was deeply creased, and gray hair showed from under his cap. He was an older man.

The next year, a different truck arrived loaded with loose coal. Two younger men, with straighter backs, set up a chute with a conveyor belt system powered by a kerosene engine. They swiftly shoveled the coal onto the moving conveyor belt. The conveyor fed the coal from the street, alongside the house and through the window of the coal room. After a couple of hours, the coal room was full.

I wondered what happened to the bent-over, old man. I hoped he had the new system and he didn't have to work so hard anymore.

Naomi bought an electric clothes washer with a powered wringer that got the water out of the clothes much better than my wringing them by hand had. I was careful to not let the laundry bunch up between the two wooden rollers and stall the machine. I worked frantically to untangle the sheets as the rollers relentlessly pulled on them. If I broke her new machine, Naomi would kill me. I moved quickly to prevent my fingers getting caught between the rollers. I didn't want crushed-flat fingers. At times, I feared the rollers would grab my hands and pull my entire body through and spit me out into the tub of rinse water. I'd be a flattened and dead, laundry boy.

I still had to wash some of the laundry by hand on the scrub board, but washing clothes was less laborious now and took less of my time. Plenty of other work occupied that void, except when Naomi was disorganized. Then, I spent more hours alone in my room. My life with Naomi was either exhausting labor or painful isolation.

During canning season, I worked from early morning until late in the night. In addition to the large purchases Naomi made from a produce wagon, next-door-neighbor Margaret gave her some of the extra from her highly productive garden.

For endless hours, shrouded in mists of steam, I peeled, cut and boiled vegetables and fruit. I filled and sealed mason jars. The process took up both the kitchen and the basement. Again and again, I ran up and down the steps to the basement carrying food and jars.

Finally, the shelves in the basement were filled with numbered and dated glass containers of infinite shapes and sizes. Naomi kept a list of each jar stored on the shelves down there, and the fury of the devil would fall upon me if any were broken or went missing. As I tended to the furnace, labored over laundry, and maintained rat traps in the basement, I was surrounded by hundreds of jars of food, but severe punishment awaited me if I dared to steal and feast on the contents of even one of those glass containers.

Naomi allowed a certain amount of time for each job to be completed to her satisfaction. If I worked fast and achieved perfection, I had a few minutes to claim as my own. During those wonderful respites, I found a warm spot in the basement and sat quietly. I tried not to think about the current condition of my life. I stared at a soft shaft of light that penetrated the basement window's layer of grime. That beam illuminated minute particles of dust that appeared to be dancing a glorious ballet. Entranced, I watched this soothing performance and imagined a magical world without fear and pain. I escaped to a life that offered lots of delicious food and even tiny bits of human kindness.

If the dogs were interested, I played fetch with them. Many times, I pulled them onto my lap and hugged them close to my body. Even Manny, the grouchy terrier, had grown to like me.

I was struggling through my second winter of bondage to Naomi. I trudged to school after a heavy snowfall. The snow in Chicago wasn't ever truly white. In its fall from the clouds, the snow mixed with the pall of smoke that hung over the city. The flakes of soot from all the coal furnaces that heated apartment buildings, factories, and high-rises, married the snowflakes on their way down from the sky. On the ground, the snow turned into a dirty slush. The snowmen that kids built looked as if they'd been sprinkled with black pepper. Naomi forced me to steal enough tins of black pepper and other seasonings to cover many snowmen.

It was a freezing cold day, but I was grateful to reach my classroom safely. I hadn't been waylaid by any hard punches or cruel trips from the bullies.

"We're going to have an air raid drill," the teacher announced. "When the siren sounds, get down on your knees next to your desk. Put your hands over your head and put your elbows on your desk seat. Use your desk for cover. It will protect you from the bomb blast."

The school staged these drills monthly. The siren began its long wail. We children scrambled into the position as instructed. We hoped we'd be safe when the Russians dropped an atomic bomb on top of us.

Personally, I worried about surviving the bullies who stalked the playground and my walk to and from school. Their humiliating words and brutal fists scared me far more than the threat of being roasted alive by radiation.

During a school assembly, the principal showed a film which shouted about the danger we faced. The booming voice told us what to do when an atomic bomb exploded. If you were outside, in the open, you were supposed to fall down and cover your head when you saw the bright flash in the sky. If you were at home in your bedroom, you were supposed to crawl under your bed.

After a while, I did worry about the terrifying nuclear blasts. On my walk to and from school, I scanned the heavens around me. I looked for the bright lights of the many atomic bomb explosions. I imagined clouds of destruction billowing miles high into the sky. I frantically looked for places to hide.

The fear of the atomic bomb entered my dreams. *The entire skyline filled with eyeball destroying, super-bright flashes. Towering mushroom clouds rose to fill the horizon. Gigantic waves of deadly radiation rolled towards me. I was engulfed by a terrible heat. My clothes burned off, my skin peeled from my body and my screams of pain echoed for blocks.*

But gradually, I thought of the bomb in a different way. The bomb might be my friend. I wouldn't be injured because, like my hero, Superman, I had superpowers. The blast would kill all the bullies. The blast would vaporize Naomi. It might take an atomic bomb to kill her, but Naomi could be killed.

Hundreds of bombs fell. Fires raged. Radiation spread. I was the only human to survive. Manny and Max were the only dogs to survive. We three were the last living things left on this planet. We had all the hamburgers, candy bars, BB-guns and comic books to ourselves. It was a wonderful world for me and for them.

Thank you, blessed Jesus. Thank you for answering my prayers. Thank you for saving me from the Atomic bombs and thank you for letting the bombs incinerate Naomi.

As I lay asleep and dreamed, images of my mother holding me and hugging me filled my sight. I heard her say she loved me. She snuggled me tight to her body. I loved her smell and her body warmth, but something strange happened. My penis grew larger and became hard and felt ready to burst. A physical sensation, a surge of intense feeling like I hadn't ever felt before, went through me. My spine had melted, and a surge of warmth flowed through my lower body and out of the end of my penis.

I woke up. The warmth had disappeared. I shivered from a cold sweat. I felt clammy moisture at my crotch.

"Jesus," I moaned. "I'm way too old to wet my bed."

Barely awake, I crawled out from under my covers and felt for the light switch. The sudden flood of brightness shocked my eyes. Focusing, I looked into my underwear, where I expected to see yellow urine or red blood. Instead, a whitish muck coated my penis and my lower stomach.

I felt deathly ill. What horrible illness was attacking me? What was causing this disgusting stuff to come out of my body?

For days afterward, I worried I was dying from a deadly disease.

After several more of these nighttime happenings, I decided I wasn't dying from some illness. The dreams that caused the muck to erupt from my penis were much better than my usual nightmares of falling into an abyss and suffering a horrible death. Mom was back in my dreams. I lay next to her in her bed, and I molded tightly to her body. I wrapped my arms around her neck. It was just she and I, as she pulled me close to her warmth. My spine melted again and again. It was the most overwhelming sensation I'd ever felt. Night after night, hot lava flowed from my penis.

I had a new diversion. I touched myself in a way that felt good. Humping my pillow or my mattress was a rough way to get the release I needed, but at a certain point, I couldn't stop. Even if it hurt, I couldn't stop. I caused my penis to be sore for a few days, but there wasn't any possibility I'd ever quit what I was doing. It was my good luck I washed all the linens. I scrubbed the muck stains from my pillowcase, my sheets, and my underwear. If Naomi discovered what I was doing, she'd surely cut my penis off with one of her sharpest kitchen knives and throw it into the garbage.

I was eleven-years-old, but I hadn't grown much since I'd lived with Naomi. I worried that something was wrong with me. Is it the stuff I'd have been forcing out of my penis? Do I have to stop doing that if I was ever going to grow up strong and healthy? What about when I was asleep, and it happened during my dreams? I couldn't stop that. Anyway, I wouldn't stop doing it because it was the only good thing that ever happened to me.

I did worry I was committing a terrible sin. Would I end up in hell for making myself feel good? Could Jesus see me? Was he watching me each time I abused myself? Was Jesus shaking his head at me with disgust like Naomi always did?

Chapter 24

Manny, the terrier, was fourteen-years-old and having difficulty climbing up and down the steps and making his way out to the backyard. I half-carried and half-dragged him out to the small patch of grass. When I got him there, he only wanted to lie down. He didn't want to stand up to do his business.

"Manny has to stay in the basement from now on," Naomi grumbled. "That dog is dying from old age. There's nothing anyone can do for him. You'd better not fall behind in your work because of that dog. You can't carry him everywhere. I don't want you wasting your time with him."

I hated Naomi so much. Most of the time, my hatred for her made me feel sick.

I made a bed out of old sheets near the furnace so Manny would have a warm place to lie. He and I were best friends now. I sat with him as often as I could sneak time away from my busy work schedule. Sad-eyed Max, the basset hound, lay quietly a small distance away and stared at us. The two dogs and I listened to the comforting sounds that came from the furnace. Sparks popped and burnt cinders settled into place. The stoker motor kicked in and sent new coal to the base of the fire. Clinkers rose and fell. More sparks popped. But there were also upsetting sounds. Above us, support timbers and flooring creaked as Naomi's lumbered from room to room. Water pipes shuddered throughout the house as the monster turned faucets on and off.

Manny quit eating his food and drinking his water. I hand fed him little bits of food and dripped water onto his tongue. When he did his business lying down, I cleaned up the mess, and I cleaned him up. He was embarrassed, so I didn't make a fuss about cleaning him up.

Manny liked to be held by me now. I really enjoyed the feel of his warm, living body. He allowed me to pull him close so he could rest his head on my lap. He was brave. I wouldn't ever let anyone hold me that close. What if they decided to hit you? You'd be defenseless.

Manny wheezed and struggled to breathe. I cried tears for both of us.

I liked the time in the basement with the dying dog. I especially liked when we turned off most of the lights and sat in near total darkness. The wavering orange glow from the furnace was the main illumination. Manny rested his head in my lap and, occasionally, looked up into my eyes. He appeared to understand how lucky he was he didn't have to die alone. The red flames from the furnace were reflected in his large, brown eyes. I cried more tears.

Max and I came down to the basement the fourth morning after Manny had quit eating on his own. As we approached him, I sensed the worst. Manny was breathless, stiff and cold.

Poor Manny had died alone.

I let Max out into the yard. I went back up to the kitchen to tell Naomi the terrible news.

"Manny is dead." I held back my tears that wanted to flow like a waterfall.

"Get rid of him. Put him in the trash can."

"Put him in the trash can?"

"That's right. Put him in the trash can."

"Can't I bury him in the garden?"

Naomi closed in on me. "I told you to throw him into the trash can. Quit arguing with me."

"But—"

Slap!

"Ow!" I was so disconcerted by Manny's death I hadn't been ready for her slap. She hit me on my cheek with all her force. I staggered backwards and almost fell. My usual reaction when the monster hit me was to cringe to the floor and curl into a protective ball. But this time I stayed upright. My face felt hot as if I'd been burned with fire. I was sure my cheek had turned red and showed her brutish handprint. I bet that gave the devil lots of satisfaction. The times I instinctively raised my arms to protect my face from her blows made her more furious. She'd double her assault and break through my defense. She became doubly enraged when she hurt her hands by hitting my hard, bony arms, rather than my face.

I couldn't control the hate that radiated from my eyes. I wanted to strike back. I wanted to kill her. She still held her fist up, as if she was going to hit me again, but a flash of doubt showed on the beast's face. Her eyes showed uncertainty. Her expression showed caution as if even she realized there was a limit to the punishment I'd endure without fighting back. I looked at the sharp bread knife lying on the kitchen table. I almost lunged towards that blade. With difficulty, I stopped myself. Rather than grabbing the deadly knife and plunging it deep into her big body, I turned away and forced myself to go down to the basement to do the sickening task she demanded of me.

Let the monster grab me from behind, I thought. Let her. Then, I will pick up that long, sharp knife and stick it deep into her throat.

I hoped she'd attack me again. My red-hot rage prayed for relief through revenge.

I staggered down the steps to the basement. My heart was crushed over Manny's death. A horrible hatred of Naomi and most humans flowed through me. I wanted to hit one of the world's biggest bullies and send him flying backwards through the air. I wanted to scream out in my loudest voice and shatter millions of windows. I wanted to plunge a knife deep into my enemies' necks and twist and watch their blood spurt out, flooding the earth just like God flooded the world for Noah and his ark.

Manny lay on the bed I put together for him. His eyes were open. His teeth were half-exposed by the curl of his lips. I'd seen that death look before. There were plenty of dead cats and dead rats and even an occasional dead dog in the filthy alleys of Chicago. Those animals had the same awful look of death. Most of them were covered with crawling maggots, and they reeked. I didn't want to think about filthy maggots and putrid death odor on Manny.

I was afraid to pick him up. I didn't want to touch his stiff, dead body. I found an old, paint-splattered, half-sheet and wrapped it around him. I half-carried and half-dragged Manny up the narrow staircase for the last time. I hated myself each time I bumped poor Manny as I struggled upwards. This last trip wasn't to the garden to be buried with dignity. Manny's last journey was to the trash can.

Manny was heavy, even though he'd faded to a virtual skeleton. Once outside, Max cautiously followed us. He sniffed at the strange bundle I dragged across the yard. Finally, I was next to Manny's final resting place. I took the lid off the trash can. Manny was as rigid as a thick, wood plank and it was difficult for me to lift him and fit him into the trash can. Carefully, I wedged him in. I didn't want to break his legs and hear the sound of his bones cracking. Please, Lord Jesus. Not that.

For three days, I piled garbage on top of Manny, pushing him closer to the bottom of the can. The stench worsened. The thought of maggots crawling out of Manny's mouth made me heartsick. I should have done more for him. I should have killed Naomi so Manny could have had a decent burial.

As I piled more garbage on top of him, I also feared Manny would come back to life. He'd claw his way up through the stinking garbage and foaming at his mouth, he'd leap from the trash can, and attack me like a rabid mongrel. Hell. Manny had every right to be violently angry with me. I failed him completely.

I hid nearby and listened as the garbage men made their weekly pickup, but I didn't dare watch them empty our garbage cans.

After they left, I checked the two metal containers. Manny was gone. I stepped into the alley and watched the garbage truck rumble off into the distance. I wiped tears and snot on my shirtsleeve. Goodbye, Manny.

Damn. I hated Naomi. I hated myself.

Soon after Manny died, I found the canary dead at the bottom of its cage. I'd grown to love the bird. I'd put my hand into his cage and hold my finger out to him. He worked up his courage and hopped on my offered finger. As long as I didn't try to remove him from his cage, he perched happily on my finger and groomed himself. He trusted me and sang beautiful songs to me.

It was difficult to reach in his cage and pick up his lifeless body. Stiff and cold in death, his bright yellow feathers were still soft, and his tiny-boned body felt weightless in my hand.

I stood in front of Naomi and showed her the dead bird.

"The canary died," I said. It was her bird, but she didn't act like she cared at all. In fact, I never saw her care about anything except her damn money.

"Well," she glared at me. "You must not have taken very good care of him."

"I thought I did." I knew I tried my best to properly care for him. Canaries are fragile birds, and the slightest cold draft could kill them.

"Throw it in the trash can. Clean up the cage and put in the basement. I'm not going to spend any more money on birds."

The monster wasn't watching me when I went out to the backyard. I quickly dug a small hole in a corner of the garden. I smoothed out the bird's feathers, laid him neatly in his grave and carefully covered him with earth. I prayed he'd go to heaven and see Manny there.

Damn tears. Why was I crying over a stupid, little, yellow bird?

Chapter 25

One day, Naomi had me on my hands and knees planting flowers in the backyard. She stood over me supervising as I dug in the moist, black soil. I glanced up and saw a figure turn off the front sidewalk and approach us. The girl, who appeared to be around fifteen, stopped several feet from Naomi and me. She was just over five-feet-tall, with dull brown hair, and wore a shirtwaist dress that showed too much leg. She radiated fear and apprehension.

"Mama," She moaned. Naomi stiffened and glared venom at her. I stopped digging and watched.

"What do you want?" Naomi screeched. I looked from the girl to Naomi. Anger and hatred distorted Naomi's features. It was as scary as any evil face she'd directed at me.

The girl clasped her hands in front of her and twisted them together so fiercely they turned white.

"Mama, I want to come home." She forced the words out in a weak, frightened voice. Tears welled in the corners of her eyes.

"You'll never come back here!" Naomi's false teeth clacked menacingly.

I stood up, transfixed by the scene.

"Mama, I want to see Papa."

"Get away from here, you filthy whore!"

The girl flinched as if she'd been slapped across the face. "Please Mama." Tears coursed down her face.

"Get away from here, or I'll call the police on you. You're nothing but a thieving slut."

The girl backed away, cowering like a rejected stray dog that had only wanted a tiny scrap of food.

I looked at her exposed legs again. I wondered if a girl so young could really be a slut and a whore.

"Please, Mama." Her voice was barely audible - the last distress call from a drowning swimmer.

"Go away!" Naomi shouted at the top of her voice. "I took you in, and you stole from me, you ungrateful bitch."

"I'm sorry, Mama." The girl retreated several more steps.

"You'll never come back here to live, you worthless trash. I don't want to ever see you again."

"Mama," a last plaintive word squeezed out of her. Hunched over and defeated, the girl turned and staggered away. The sound of her crying faded away. I heard a crow call out sharply. Even the birds had turned against her.

"That damn bitch stole one of my rings," Naomi spit out. She turned and glared at me accusingly. "Be generous to children and look what they do to you."

Suddenly, I felt terrible guilt. I stole money from Naomi's coin purse. I stole bits of food I found around her house and tried to avoid some of the work she forced on me. After all, Naomi had done for me, I was defiant and wanted to inflict horrible pain on her. She provided me with a home when nobody else in the world wanted me, and I hated her. Naomi appeared to be reading my mind. Her eyes stared a deadly warning at me. Did she know how much I hated her, and how desperately I wanted to escape? Did she know how much I wanted to kill her? I looked down at my feet.

"Get back to work," she yelled and stormed off to the house.

What was so wicked out in the world that made this girl want to come back to this place and be with Naomi? Whatever her age, she seemed like a child. Was she really a slut and a whore? Was she a girl who was easy to have sex with? That confusing fever coursed through me and I felt more terrible guilt.

It was difficult for me to believe the scene I'd just witnessed had really happened. The girl was real. She was a breathing, sobbing mass of pain. I wanted to hear her story. We could compare our pain. There was a chance she might hate me because I'd taken her place. My prison cell might have been her room. Had she slept in the bed I now sleep in. She didn't seem to notice me at all during her exchange with Naomi. She probably wouldn't want to hear my stupid story. She was gone now. It wouldn't do me any good if she was a whore and a slut.

In the solitude of my room, I thought about the girl. I remembered her legs, and I thought about what was under her skirt. I thought about the sex things she might have done. I masturbated until I was sorer than ever before, I tried to stop my sinful thoughts. I tried to stop my body, but awake or asleep, I couldn't stop the overwhelming need for release from my dammed-up tension. I hated myself and wished I was dead.

Naomi gave Max to another family.

"It's not worth the bother to keep only one dog. Max was lonely without Manny around."

Naomi understood loneliness? Damn. What about me? Max had been my last, best friend.

There were rare times, usually on weekends, when Emil and Naomi went on a day trip. I used the bathroom just before they left and then climbed up the stairway to spend another day in the solitude of my room.

I stared at my walls and ceiling.

I read the Bible and Pilgrims Progress.

I staged bloody battles on my bed with the button armies.

I lay against the door and spied on the people who lived in the apartment next to me.

I watched the world pass by outside my window.

I humped my pillow.

I felt terrible guilt, slept fitfully, and dreamed horrible dreams.

Chapter 26

Once, Naomi decided I could go with her and Emil on an outing rather than stay behind in my room. I had no idea why I was given that incredible gift.

Naomi never drove an automobile and never intended to, so that task fell to Emil. I had the back seat to myself and was mostly safe from the monster.

The world changed dramatically as we left the denseness of Chicago behind. The sky got larger and green fields spread to the horizon. Houses and barns occasionally appeared amidst the vast expanses of corn and wheat. Herds of grazing cows and sheep brought life to the surrounding countryside. I turned back and forth constantly to see the wonders on both sides of the road. I barely believed I was in an automobile, cruising along a country highway.

"Quit bouncing around back there," the monster yelled. She turned part way around to glare at me. The effort made her gasp for air. I pressed myself against the back seat so the beast couldn't reach me. The devil didn't have enough space to maneuver and get close enough to punch me. Until the car stopped, I was safe from her punishments.

"Here we are," Emil said with a sigh of relief. He sounded tired from driving. I wanted to believe he also hated being stuck in the front seat with his stinking, ugly wife.

They owned a two-story house, on one acre of land, a couple of hours drive outside of Chicago, which they rented to a family. The wood-frame farmhouse had a metal roof and a wrap-around porch, a detached two-car garage, a couple of storage sheds and a chicken coop. All the structures were painted white, and the spacious grounds were neat and orderly. This lovely little place stood at the intersection of two country roads, and as we pulled up the gravel driveway, the family of renters walked down from the porch. Three young girls, who looked to be around three to seven-years-old, hid behind the father and mother as we parked. Naomi and Emil got out of the car and greeted the adults. I stood next to the car as the girls stared at me with their big eyes showing caution and wonder. In my oversized, old-man clothes, I guess I looked truly odd like I might be a dangerous murderer. Their mother, who was pretty, wore a plain, loose-fitting dress and no makeup. She gave me a friendly smile, and I instantly imagined she might want a boy like me to keep as her own, but just as quickly, I realized I was much too old and raggedy for her to want to adopt me.

The hell with all that garbage. Today, I didn't care one-bit what humans thought of me. The family of renters didn't appear to be mean people. Not even the tall, muscular father looked or acted like a cruel bully who liked to beat kids.

The country smells of grass, corn, and farm animals were a wonderful balm for my angry mind.

Across from the intersection of the two rural roads, lived an elderly farm couple who were friends of Naomi and Emil. They invited us to visit and stay for dinner. Naomi, who didn't like the outdoors, stayed inside the modest one-story farmhouse to gossip with the farm woman. I was allowed to wander about their property freely, while Emil strolled and chatted with the farmer.

There must have been at least thirty loose chickens pecking at the ground. A dangerous looking rooster puffed up and scratched in the dirt with his powerful claws, sending up little clouds of dust. He scared me, so I went to visit the pigs. They crowded against the wooden slats that imprisoned them, grunted in unison, and looked me over with their beady little eyes. They smelled bad, so I didn't give them much of my valuable time.

"We need to pick out dinner," the old farmer said loudly. He wanted to make sure I heard him. He gave me a look that clearly meant, "Watch this, city boy!"

He grabbed the plumpest hen that wandered within his reach. His gnarled hand held the clueless creature just below her head. He twirled the red feathered body in a few quick circles and expertly wrung the unsuspecting chicken's neck. He took the not quite dead creature to a tree stump that served as a chopping block. He picked up the ax that leaned against it and with one well-aimed swing, he sent the chicken's head flying and blood spurting. He dropped the headless body onto the ground, and the hen flopped about in her final death spasms. Staring right at me, the eyes of the severed head opened and closed several times before glazing over. The other chickens went through a momentary group flutter, but quickly settled down and continued pecking at the ground. The flock forgot about their just-killed companion.

I sat at the table with the four adults and ate the same food they did. There was lots of fried chicken, mashed potatoes, gravy, fresh-shelled peas and homemade cornbread with butter. I ate and ate and ate as the elderly farm couple praised my appetite. Naomi gave me one more angry look from her endless supply.

I didn't have to wash dishes here, nor would I be sent up to my room after eating. Instead, I went outside and sat on the porch steps and petted the couple's shaggy, old farm dog. The dog smelled almost as bad as the pigs, but he really liked me and crowded against me as I scratched behind his ears.

As we drove home, Naomi's dissatisfaction radiated from the front seat. Darkness fell, and, safe in the back seat, I dozed off and enjoyed the fullest belly I'd known in a long time.

Chapter 27

Naomi loved to hoard money. She kept her coin purse on the top of her mirrored dresser. I often stole coins from her stash, and she didn't notice the missing money. I was risking my life by stealing from the monster, but I couldn't resist the temptation.

With the stolen loot, I bought a few comic books and snuck them up to my room. Superman, Batman, and Captain Marvel were my favorites. They were the superheroes I wanted to be. Alone, in my room, I imagined I had tremendous powers, and I'd beat all the bullies to death with my bare fists. I'd beat Naomi to death with my bare fists.

I still read the Bible. I forged forward through many difficult words. I read the stories about Jesus. I liked the son of God a lot, but I couldn't erase my hate and desire for revenge. Deep in my gut, I believed more in the heroes in comic books than in the bible. Comic book heroes show no mercy for their enemies.

Naomi owned a decorative Easter egg that sat on her fireplace mantle. It had a viewing hole at one end which showed an elaborate winter scene of people skating on a frozen pond. Candy-like decorations covered the outside. Recklessly, I stole her egg. I broke it with a hammer and tried to eat the small pieces. Even though it had looked delicious, it tasted awful. I spit out what I hadn't swallowed and hid what was left in a dark corner of the basement.

"What happened to my egg?"

"I don't know."

"Did you break it, you clod!"

"I didn't do anything to it." I wasn't a good liar. I wasn't a smart thief either.

"Don't lie to me. You stole it!"

She grabbed me by my hair and twisted with all her strength and slapped me hard on my face.

"Aaah!" I tried to pull free from her grasp. My efforts to escape added to the pain searing across my scalp.

"Don't you ever steal from me, you filthy little monster."

"I didn't touch your egg," I lied.

Damn her to hell. My scalp really stung.

I'd lived with Naomi for three years. There weren't ever any pork chops for me to eat. There wasn't ever roast beef, fried eggs, fried potatoes, chocolate cake or milk allowed for me. She did feed me crusts from her home-baked bread, which I liked. Boiled potatoes, carrots, and turnips were allowed. Jesus Christ. I hated boiled carrots and turnips. There was the ugly-yellow, cornmeal-gruel every morning for breakfast. At times, there was extra boiled rhubarb from the pies she baked for Emil and herself and the rubbery top of the butterscotch pudding. I always wanted more than Naomi gave me, but I learned not to ask. I stole bits of food whenever the opportunity arose, and I prayed she wouldn't catch me.

I wasn't allowed to celebrate Christmas. I wasn't allowed to celebrate Thanksgiving. I wasn't allowed to celebrate the Fourth of July or Easter or any other holiday. I wasn't allowed to celebrate my birthdays.

The monster did allow me to go out to trick-or-treat one Halloween night. It was an unexpected and frightening gift of freedom. I wore my regular raggedy, oversized, old-man clothes and she darkened my face with charcoal, so I looked like a little colored boy.

People who answered my knock and opened their doors to me were quite impressed.

"Come see the raggedy, little colored boy, honey. He has blond hair and blue eyes!"

I didn't worry about running into any real coloreds on the streets, because none lived close to our Garfield Park neighborhood. Otherwise, I'd probably have been beaten to a bloody pulp and had my throat slit. Instead, I had a wonderful outing. I walked miles of familiar, unfamiliar, and sometimes frightening streets. I walked along dark hallways and knocked on dozens of doors. My shopping bag gradually filled with candy and required all my strength to carry it home along the mostly deserted, late-night streets.

I anticipated punishment because I stayed out so late. Instead, Naomi was quite impressed with my haul of free stuff. She picked out her favorites from my loot and left me more sweets than I dreamed possible.

I gorged on candy until I threw up. She didn't see me puke, so I kept eating until I vomited again. Too soon, my treasure was all gone.

"Did you eat all of that candy, you pig! I hope you get really sick."

For more than three years, I'd spied on the world from my bedroom window. I kept track of two brothers who lived down the street. One was my age, and the other was two-years older. They played catch with their friends. They rode their bicycles recklessly and wrestled each other roughly. They laughed a lot and swore a lot. They ate candy bars and drank sodas they bought at the corner market. That was the sort of stuff I did with my two older brothers, so long ago, when I lived with my real family. I was sure, at this very moment, my brothers were out on the streets of Chicago, having the same kind of fun as the two brothers down the block. Thinking about what I was missing made me tear up.

At school and during my walk to and from, the two brothers and their friends threw me on the ground and punched me. Whenever they saw me working outside the house, they cursed and ridiculed me.

A small bookkeeping company, several blocks down the street, ran an ad in the local newspaper looking for janitor services. Naomi applied for and got the job.

Five nights a week, at seven o'clock, after Emil was fed and off to bed, she and I went to work.

The office was one large room with twenty desks, two smaller offices for the bosses and two bathrooms. It took until ten o'clock to finish the cleaning. I did most of the work, with constant nagging and confusing instructions from the cow.

At home, Naomi couldn't endure much physical activity before she grew tired and short of breath and collapsed into the largest chair. The three-block walk from our house to the office wore her out, and once there, she plopped into one of their most comfortable chairs and ordered me about. It irritated her I wasn't big and strong enough to clean the office faster.

The toughest part of the job was waxing the floor on Friday nights. I stacked all the chairs and wastebaskets on the desks, then mopped and waxed the expanse of linoleum. I struggled to wring out the heavy mop and push it across the floor. I struggled to apply the wax evenly. I could barely control the electric buffing machine. I feared that damn machine was going to spin around and toss me against a wall smashing my bones to smithereens. Still, I achieved a perfect shine, and I was impressed by what I accomplished. That work kept us at the office until midnight. With this added to my work at home, my days were painfully exhausting.

More and more Naomi walked me to the office, unlocked the door, set me to work and went home for a couple of hours. Her greedy grip on this job only lasted a few months. Shortly after she left one Friday night, the front door opened, and three adults walked in.

I struggled to maneuver the floor buffer as they stared at me.

"Where's Mrs. Johnson?" said a big man wearing a suit.

I turned the machine off. "She'll be right back, sir." I wiped sweat from my forehead. Oh shit, I thought. I'm really in trouble.

"Are you doing all this work by yourself, son?"

"Yes, sir. I usually do. It's real easy for me."

"How old are you?"

"I'm twelve, sir."

He looked concerned.

"I enjoy the work, sir." I wanted to make him feel better. Mostly, I hoped to avoid Naomi's rage.

Naomi didn't beat me specifically for losing her the janitorial job and the money she cherished more than anything else in the world. Her hatred of me grew no matter what I did. I realized that would never change.

I now understood I'd always be Naomi's house slave. I'd never go out and play. I'd be isolated in my room. I'd be dressed like a freak, and Naomi would beat me forever.

Chapter 28

Emil usually took the bus to work. Except for rare weekend drives, their black 1947 DeSoto sedan sat idly in their garage.

They planned a week-long vacation and needed to ready the car for the trip. Wasps had taken up residence in a thick, wool rug lying across the hood and were busy building a nest in its folds.

"Move the rug and clean up the car," Naomi ordered.

"I'm afraid of wasps," I protested feebly.

The beast slapped me along the side of my head. Damn. "Don't come back into the house until you're done," she yelled. "And that car better be spotless."

I entered the dark garage and stopped dead in my tracks when I heard the loud drone of wasps. The swarm flew back and forth from the rug to an opening in the eaves of the roof.

What was I going to do? Crazy, crazy me acted without thinking. I grabbed the dusty, brown rug and pulled with all my strength. The drone of the wasps changed to a high-pitched roar. My hair stood on end like a person electrocuted. I dragged the rug behind me as I flew through the garage door. I threw the rug away on the grass and ran for the house as fast as I could.

The swarm grew louder as it chased me. I stumbled over my shoes and fell to my knees. The wasps surrounded me. Their stings seared my neck and face. In a full panic, I stood up and raced for the house. I squeezed past the screen door and into the back porch. A couple of wasps made it in with me. I pushed open the kitchen door and stumbled inside slamming the door behind me. The hair on my head still stood straight up, and I gasped for breath. The stings from the wasps burned like fire-hot needles. Dear God. Please help me.

"What are you doing back here so soon, you idiot? Why did you slam the door?"

"The wasps came after me," I moaned. "They stung me a bunch of times."

"Can't you ever do anything right?"

"They hurt me really bad."

She grabbed me roughly by my shoulder, pulled me over to the kitchen table and pushed me down into a chair. She impatiently pulled out the stingers and poured alcohol on the rapidly swelling, red lumps. The pain was excruciating. Please don't send me back outside to be attacked again, I prayed. They'll sting me to death. Please have mercy. Please.

"Get back to work on the wash," she screeched. "You are so useless."

Despite the intense pain, I happily went to work washing the baskets of laundry.

That night, Emil poured gasoline on the nest lying on the grass. He lit a match and set the ball of terror on fire. I watched from the back porch as the insects and their nest were consumed in a rush of flames. I loved the crackle of their burning bodies.

The next morning, surviving wasps buzzed around me as I carried buckets of water to the garage and washed the DeSoto. The insects kept me in constant fear, but I either faced them, or I faced Naomi.

Emil's boss gave them the use of the guesthouse at his wooded, twenty-acre estate two-hours northwest of Chicago. Naomi and Emil had to take me along, so the three of us set out on the road.

I had the back seat to myself and was out of hitting range. I relaxed and looked forward to this one-week vacation. Other than the time I was sick and close to dying, it would be my longest break in more than three years from my constant slavery to housework. I wouldn't have to shoplift for Naomi for an entire week. I wouldn't have to shuffle my way to the store while avoiding packs of neighborhood bullies. For an entire week, I wouldn't have to face the numbing isolation of my room.

I watched the passing farmland and deep-green forests. I dozed off and on, but it was difficult to forget the wasp attack. I could still hear the horrifying buzz as they pursued me. The places they stung me were healing but itched terribly. I found it impossible not to scratch.

"This is it," Emil said.

We turned onto a rough and bouncy gravel road and drove between two decorative brick columns designed to be a grand entryway. Densely treed grounds surrounded us.

The single-story, stucco guesthouse impressed me plenty. Then I saw the main house, a large, two-story, granite-block mansion with tall, arched windows that revealed glimpses of rich furnishings.

The greenery covering the estate looked untended and resembled a wild forest. After I helped carry our luggage into the guesthouse, I slipped out of Naomi's sight.

At first, I stayed within view of the buildings as I explored the wilderness. From the edge of the dense undergrowth and trees, I spotted Naomi. She huffed and puffed as she walked around the main house looking through its windows and elaborate glass doors. She turned and peered in my direction.

"Mickey," she rasped as loud as her weakened voice allowed.

I stayed silent, crouched motionless and held my breath.

"Mickey. Where are you?" She strained her eyes trying to locate me.

Ha. The monster couldn't see me.

I crept deeper into the trees and brush until her voice faded. I stepped as quietly as possible. Bird songs and insect chirps filled the air. I pretended I was hunting snorting, heavily-antlered stags and evading the bloodthirsty savages and man-killing beasts that lurked in these wilds.

I found a hiding spot next to a large tree trunk. I burrowed in as comfortably as I could against the tall tree. Birds warbled and called to each other. They flew from tree to tree and hopped about in the undergrowth. I hoped to see a passing deer and a sleek, black panther stalking it. I stayed as quiet as the best Indian scout in the movies. I resisted the urge to smash a shiny-black beetle that crawled over my shoe. I felt good when it disappeared under a clump of leaves and continued living. At that moment, I was part of nature and free from the cruelty of the world. The exhilaration of being free made me dizzy.

I was content to be alone in the wild, except it would be more fun if I had a dog. I missed Manny and Max. These woods would be a haven for the three of us. We could roam through this magical place forever.

In the forest canopy, the leaves trembled in a light breeze. As I stared, a face formed in the maze of greenery. The image grew sharper, and loving eyes looked down at me. I blinked. I couldn't believe what I saw.

"Mom," I whispered as loud as I could without being overheard by Naomi.

The image froze. I clearly saw Mom. She looked right into my eyes. She smiled at me like she was overjoyed to see me.

"Mom. It's me. It's your son, Mickey."

She recognized me. She gazed lovingly at me but remained wordless.

I waited for her to float down and grab me in her arms. We'd fly away together. I pleaded for her to save me. Suddenly, a wind blew through the canopy, the leaves fluttered, and Mom twisted away.

"Mom, come back!"

Damn her. She left me behind. Again.

I buried my head in my crossed arms. I squeezed my eyes shut until I saw fireworks and my stomach ached. I wanted to hide deep in the ground under this tree. I wanted to stay hidden in a dark hole for the rest of my life.

Instead of being rescued by Mom, I returned to Naomi.

"I called for you, stupid. Where were you?" She slapped at my face, but I dodged a tiny bit. She hit my forehead and only scratched me with her ragged fingernails.

"Ouch. I'm sorry." I went into my frightened-cur cringe.

"Don't you ever disappear like that again."

"I'm sorry."

"You'd better come running when I call you."

"Yes, ma'am."

On the second day of our vacation, Naomi pointed out a colorful, china peacock figurine and a crystal flower vase in the main house. She said I had to steal them for her. She showed me an unlatched window she could force open wide enough for me to squeeze through. There were so many fancy things inside the mansion, I guessed she thought they wouldn't be missed.

"We'll come back here tonight after dark."

"What if I get caught?"

She grabbed me by my hair before I could dodge her. "Ouch."

"You won't get caught, stupid!"

"I'm afraid!" I couldn't escape her powerful grip.

"I'll kill you if you don't obey!" She gasped for air, and her face turned pale. She looked like she'd fall over dead if she kept pulling my hair. Her death would be my fault because I resisted her. They'd convict me, and I'd be headed for the gallows to die with my neck stretched several feet and my tongue hanging out. I'd go to hell and burn forever. Again and again, Satan would stab me with his red-hot pitchfork.

"Okay," I whined for mercy. "I'll do it."

The monster let go of my hair, and I fell to the ground.

Chapter 29

I couldn't stand any more of Naomi forcing me to wear raggedy, old-man clothes, using me as her house slave, screaming at me, hitting me, making me steal and forcing me into isolation. I was twelve-years-old, and I'd reached my limit. That afternoon, I decided to run away. If the brute tracked me down and caught me, she'd kill me, but I had to attempt an escape from her.

I walked out the long gravel driveway of the estate and left the hell of Naomi behind me. I felt hopeful, sure my victory over her was near. That feeling faded when I reached the paved road and struggled to decide which direction I should go. What a hopeless dummy I was. What chance did I have in this world full of cruel grownups and gangs of bullies? I couldn't even decide which direction to run.

I turned right and hurried along the side of the two-lane highway. When I'd put a safe distance between Naomi and me, I slowed down.

Occasional houses, set back from the road with long gravel driveways, were the only breaks in the surrounding forest. A few people in passing cars looked at me, some smiled, others just looked nosey. A creepy looking man, who was alone, slowed down and stared at me. I didn't want to be bothered by one of those. Jesus Christ. They were everywhere. I walked away from the edge of the blacktop, so people didn't think I was trying to hitch a ride. I didn't trust one single person in the whole, stinking world.

I grew bored trudging along the roadway, so I looked for deposit bottles. I only found two and quickly tired of carrying them. I hurled them into the forest. One broke against a tree trunk, which caused birds to take flight and shriek warning calls. Twitchy squirrels eyeballed me then scurried up tree trunks and chattered an alarm to the surrounding forest.

Shit. Everything and everybody was against me.

I needed real money, and most of the houses had mailboxes close to the road. I picked a story-book-style cottage that had its drapes drawn closed and looked as if nobody was awake or at home. I strolled past it a short way. I decided it was empty, and I wouldn't be seen. I went back and waited until there were no cars in sight. I flipped down the mailbox door, grabbed an envelope, stuck it under my oversized shirt and quickly walked away.

When I was out of sight of the house, I looked at my loot. It was a small, lightweight envelope. Jesus Christ, what a big-time bandit I was. I hoped there was money in it. I ripped it open and unfolded the single page it contained. It was a letter written in beautiful handwriting on flowery, sweetly-scented stationery. I read the letter as I walked on. From a woman to a man, the letter was filled with mushy words about love and forgiveness and hope for understanding. The elegant handwriting and the smell from the pages reminded me of my mother. It'd been nearly four years since Mom had given me to Naomi and she hadn't ever mailed anything to me. Didn't she care about me one tiny bit? Damn her. I read the letter again.

Dear James,

I try with all my heart to understand and be supportive, my dearest. I realize I can't ever fathom the horror of war and what you went through in Korea. I can't imagine the memories that haunt you unless you talk to me. Maybe I can help you find your way back to peace and a normal life. Please give me a chance, my love. When I look at you, I don't see a cripple. I see the man I want to spend my life with. For both our sakes, give me a chance to convince you.

I will love you forever,

Sally

Damn! The man who lives in that house must be a Korean War hero. His windows were covered up because he's a cripple and doesn't want to be seen by anyone.

I wanted to put the letter back into the mailbox but feared the hero would see me and scream at me in a tortured voice or be legless and burst out of his house on a roller board to chase me down. I hated myself for doing it, but I wadded the fancy, scented paper into a small ball and threw it as far as I could into the dense underbrush. Naomi had been right when she called me a monster. I plodded on.

Crickets started up their incessant noise as darkness approached. Thirst, hunger, and weariness slowed me down. My raggedy, old-man clothes didn't provide much warmth for my shivering body. There were fewer houses now. The forest was denser and more forbidding. Stagnant, moss-covered ponds didn't offer safe drinking water. Mosquitoes buzzed all around and bit me mercilessly. I didn't see any place that would shelter me from the cold, or where I could sleep, safe from the wild beasts that roamed at night. Noisy black crows circled above me and squawked like they were ready to attack. If I fell over and died here, those black-feathered carnivores would pick my eyeballs right out of my rotting skull.

Suddenly, flashing red and yellow lights surrounded me. The sound of tires on gravel made me turn around. A cop car pulled up alongside me. The copper pulled over to the side of the road in front of me and blocked my chance for escape. I was busted for my awful crime against the war hero and the woman who loved him. My escape from Naomi wasn't looking good either.

The officer who got out of the car was young, tall, and muscular like my comic book hero GI Joe. He was armed with a pistol in his holster and a serious look on his face.

"How're you doing, son?"

"I'm doing fine, sir," Was he going to put handcuffs on me?

"Is your name Mickey Johnson?"

"Yes, sir." My mouth was parched from lack of water and from fear.

"Your parents are really worried about you."

"They aren't my parents, sir," I protested. "I just live with those people."

I felt a surge of anger that anyone thought Naomi was my parent. If this copper knew how pretty my real mother was, he'd be impressed and apologize for his big mistake.

He kept the serious look on his face. I guessed he wanted to scare the "little runaway kid" and teach him a good lesson. What bullshit. I wasn't so scared now. Naomi had better be frightened about what I'll say to the cops. Maybe, I'll really be rescued from her, and they'll toss her into a filthy prison.

The copper let me sit in the front seat with him as he made a call back to the police station on his radio telling them he'd found the runaway kid. As I admired all the great cop stuff in his car, including the sawed-off shotgun and the multi-colored lights flashing on his radio, I told him why I'd run away.

"Naomi was going to make me steal stuff from the mansion where we were visiting, and she was going to beat me if I didn't obey her. She always makes me steal, and she always hits me. She makes me do housework and wash laundry. She won't let me have any friends. My mother left me with her when I was nine-years-old. I'm twelve now, and Mom hasn't visited me once." I didn't talk about the bullies at school, because then he'd think I was a total sissy.

"You haven't heard from your mother or any of your family for more than three years?"

"No, sir. It's almost four years. I haven't talked to any of them at all."

"It's hard to believe anyone can be as mean as you describe your foster mother."

"It's true, sir. I didn't want to break into that mansion and steal stuff.

And, Naomi isn't my foster mother. She's a cruel woman my mother left me with." Naomi was much worse than I described to the cop. Why are people always trying to make her into a better person than she is?

He listened, and his face showed concern.

"Stealing is a terrible thing to make a kid do." He sounded like he felt sorry for me.

"Naomi is a lot bigger than me, sir. She beats me whenever she wants to. If I try to dodge, she grabs me by my hair and hits me harder."

"We certainly need to talk to her about all this."

Wow. My rescue from Naomi could really happen. This copper believed me, and he'd fix everything.

On the way to police headquarters, which I was excited to see, we stopped and picked up ice cream cones. It was exactly what a kind police officer would do for the innocent little kids in the storybooks and the movies. Hopefully, this cop didn't know about me stealing mail from the crippled hero. I hoped he didn't know about the money I stole from Naomi's purse. I hoped he wouldn't find out about the criminal things I'd done with my brothers on the streets of Chicago and how we always had to run from the coppers.

The other police at the jailhouse acted as if they believed my story. They didn't put me in handcuffs and take my picture with a number across my chest. They didn't lock me up in a cell. Through a thick, glass partition, I watched them talk to red-faced, protesting Naomi and silent, pale-faced Emil.

I heard her muffled voice, and I read her lips. "He's a liar and a thief and a monster and his own mother didn't want him. If I hadn't given him a good home, who knows what would've happened to him. He'd be locked away in a reform school or have been murdered on the streets of Chicago! Reform school is where he belongs."

God, please don't let the cops believe her.

I hoped the police would save me. Instead, they sent me off with Emil and

Naomi. Damn them. They should have thrown her in a jail cell and beaten her with a club. The copper who picked me up didn't look me in the eye as I walked out the front door of the station. I thought he'd be a superhero and save me from the brute, Naomi. He was supposed to be a protector of helpless, innocent children. Hell. He betrayed me. He let the monster take me away. He didn't care one bit if she killed me when she had me alone.

We went back to the estate and hurriedly packed our belongings. I thought Naomi was going to explode. We left immediately for the drive back to Chicago. I prayed to be invisible. I never saw Emil so angry.

"You could have cost me my job," he sputtered at Naomi. "How could you do such a thing? Steal from my boss. Are you crazy?"

His hands were white from gripping the steering wheel so tight, and his face was flushed a scarlet-red. He trembled uncontrollably as he yelled at her. Was he going to hit her? I hoped not. If he hit her, she'd blame me, and she'd beat me to death when she had me alone.

"We need to find this boy's mother and make her take him back. He ran away just like Ruth did. You promised you wouldn't ever force another child to steal. I give you all the money I can."

The monster couldn't get any words out to counter Emil's anger.

"We can't keep this boy!" he shouted. He ran the car off the road.

Gravel sprayed and bounced against the underside of the vehicle. A cloud of dust rose as Emil struggled to get the DeSoto back on the roadway.

Naomi's breathing grew more ragged than ever before. She held her arms tightly across her chest. She looked like she was going to have a heart attack and die at any second. Her hatred enveloped me like thick smoke.

The rest of the drive back to Chicago was a terrible silence except for Emil's angry muttering, Naomi's gasping for air, and the auto tires thumping against the asphalt highway. I was trapped in the backseat of this automobile and on my way to my painful, bloody death.

Chapter 30

After what felt like forever, we arrived home from our shortened vacation. Emil angrily slammed his door shut as he exited the car. Naomi struggled mightily to pull herself out through her door. I fled into the house and up to my room before the beast could grab me. Cowering with fear, I sat on the floor of my room at the end of my bed. Hoping to be invisible, I crouched as low as I could and listened for the sound of the monster's thundering footsteps on the stairway as she came up after me. I didn't want to think about her revenge on me, but thoughts of the different ways she'd kill me flooded my mind. She might beat me to death with her fists and her walking stick. She might slice my head off with a kitchen knife. The thought of her stabbing me all over my body with a long, sharp knife scared me the most.

What could I do? If she didn't kill me tonight, I might get a chance to kill her tomorrow.

Would the police arrest me, even after I told them about all the terrible things she did to me? Who'd ever believe me? The copper who picked me up alongside the road acted like he believed me, then he didn't believe me when we got to the police station, and Naomi started spewing her lies. The people who lived in the apartment next to my room knew how cruel she was, but would they tell the police the truth, or would they still be afraid of losing their place to live? Probably everyone would say Naomi had been kind to me. Lots of people thought I was lucky she gave me a home after my own mother didn't want me anymore. If I killed her, I'd surely be sentenced to a horrible death.

Getting rid of Naomi's big body was the only way I'd get away with killing her. I could stuff her corpse into the furnace and break it up with the poker as it charred to a crisp. I could then clean her ashes out of the bottom of the furnace and bury them in the garden. People would think she just disappeared. A dead Naomi would be too much for me to lift up and squeeze into the furnace and there wasn't any way she'd fit through the furnace door. Even though I hated the sight of other people's blood, I realized I'd have to cut her up into sections like they sliced up cows at the slaughterhouse. I'd need to cut off her arms, her legs, and her head and throw them into the furnace separately. I might even have to cut what was left of her big body into two halves. Cutting Naomi into smaller pieces would be the most sickening job I'd ever done.

If I didn't kill her, I'd have to run away again. I needed to escape before Naomi killed me.

I listened for the sound of her heavy footsteps plodding up the stairway. I waited for my door to crash open, and for her to rush at me with a razor-sharp, carving knife in her hand.

Nothing terrible happened. It remained deathly quiet.

I crawled under the covers and remembered the girl, Ruth, and the way she cried and how brutally Naomi rejected her. There must be something worse than Naomi out in the world. Why else would Ruth want to live with the monster again? Would I survive better than Ruth had on the streets of Chicago? At least I wouldn't be forced into being a slut and whore like she'd become. I only needed to stay away from the men who stalked young boys,

Jesus Christ. Whenever I thought about Ruth, my penis got bigger and really hard. Aah. It felt good to hump my pillow. I'd stop if I heard Naomi climbing up the stairs to kill me. Aaah. I hoped the people next door didn't hear me. Aaah. Ruth. No. Mom. Stay out of my thoughts, Mom. Aaah. God, please don't make me die. A bolt of electricity coursed down my lower spine and a flood of muck erupted from my penis.

After I calmed down, I felt terribly depressed. I hated myself for giving in to my filthy thoughts and my filthy habit. Mercifully, I dozed off.

The sound of heavy breathing and the clomping of footsteps on the stairway that led up to my room woke me. Raging Naomi flung the door open and thundered into my sanctuary that had turned into a trap. My bed, where I lay trembling with fear, rapidly tilted. I scrambled and clawed to climb up the mattress to escape from the monster. I had to get over the top of the mattress before she killed me. She grabbed one of my ankles with one of her big hands. Her other hand was balled up into a huge fist. She hit me with the fist she wore her large diamond ring on. Her ring broke through my skin and left a large hole in my back. I felt my blood spurt out like water spraying from a fire hydrant. I felt more searing pain on my back as she punched me again and again. She made many more holes for my blood to gush from. My screams of agony made my throat burn. Now she was slicing my legs with a long, sharp knife. She stabbed me again and again. My blood splattered across the walls of my room. Soon, the monster was standing in an ankle-deep pool of my red blood. I heard her gasp for breath.

"You bastard!" she screamed. "You are such a worthless bastard. I told you I'd kill you."

I frantically reached up towards the top of the mattress. I lost my grip and fell backwards. I fell and fell without end. I screamed for help until my throat was dry and no more sounds came out.

I startled awake. I was clammy from sweat. I struggled to focus my eyes. My mattress was flat, and I lay on my stomach. I reached back to feel my terrible wounds. I didn't feel any holes in my skin. I looked for blood on my fingertips, but there wasn't any. I hadn't bled gallons and gallons of my own dark-red blood and flooded my room.

I prayed I didn't have to face Naomi and her rage until morning. The thought of that confrontation terrified me, but I was too exhausted to keep worrying. I went back to sleep.

Chapter 31

The wail of a siren woke me. It was bright morning. Rubbing sleep from my eyes, I walked over to my window. Orange and red lights twirled and flashed atop an ambulance in front of the house. I dressed and hurried downstairs just in time to see Naomi carried out the front door on a stretcher. Two men in white jackets and pants, strained from the heavy weight of her as they awkwardly maneuvered the stretcher down the porch steps. They slid the stretcher and the monster through the wide-open back doors of the ambulance. They helped pale-faced Emil climb into the ambulance after her. The attendants slammed the back doors shut and rushed to their front seats. The siren screamed as the ambulance sped off. They disappeared into the distance, and the noise level returned to the familiar hum of autos, delivery trucks and city buses.

I stood on the front porch confused for a minute. Slowly, reality returned, and I went back into Emil and Naomi's apartment. I was totally alone. I wandered into the kitchen, then back through the dining room, down the hallway, and back out the front door. I sat on the front steps. There was no one to tell me what to do. Like a ventriloquist's dummy without a hand to guide him, I just sat there. Then, my stomach rumbled to remind me I hadn't eaten any breakfast.

I went back inside to Naomi's room and found her purse sitting on the dresser. I took a one-dollar-bill and a handful of coins. I prayed the monster wouldn't notice the missing money when she came home. I went back outside and looked in both directions. After a couple of hesitations, I walked up to the corner market.

There weren't any bullies hanging around in front of the store. I strolled inside. There weren't any bullies inside the store. Now feeling confident, I bought a package of Hostess snowballs, a Baby Ruth candy bar and a Nehi orange soda.

I walked back to the house and sat on the front steps to eat my delicious breakfast.

Free from Naomi's brutal control for the first time in over three years, I barely knew how to function without her commands. What should I do next? I needed to think and act on my own. There wasn't any way I was doing my daily work until the monster returned and stood over me with her beating stick.

That evening, Emil arrived home by taxi carrying bags of deli food. He invited me to sit at the dining room table with him. We feasted on thick slices of ham, chunks of pickled herring and mouthfuls of delicious potato salad. This was the first time I sat at their fancy table. Naomi never let me sit anywhere except the kitchen table to eat the scraps she allowed me. Emil's eyes were red from crying. He looked at me and, for the first time, spoke directly to me.

"Mickey. Naomi suffered a stroke during the night," he said in a broken voice. "I didn't realize she was sick until I woke up this morning."

I had no idea what a stroke was. It surprised the hell out of me Emil knew my name. He never referred to me by anything other than "boy."

"I'm afraid I caused her to have a stroke by yelling at her so much," he said to himself, not to me. Jesus, he didn't sound mad at her anymore.

I hoped he wouldn't say it was also my fault she had the stroke because I ran away.

I wondered if it was my fault. Was the beast sick because I ran away, and the coppers had to pick me up, and I told them how she forced me to steal? Was it my fault because I constantly upset her and caused her to beat me? What if Naomi died? Would her death be my fault, because

I was a worthless slum boy who tried to avoid work and stole scraps of food? Why was I feeling so relieved and happy Naomi was sick and wasn't around to yell at and beat me? There had to be something terribly wrong with me for enjoying her illness.

Of course, there was something terribly wrong with me. My own mother had decided she didn't want me to be her child anymore. My own mother had put an advertisement in the newspaper offering me to any stranger who wanted a nine-year-old boy. My own mother had decided I wasn't good enough to be anything but a slave for a stranger. Damn my mother and damn Naomi. Everybody in the whole stinking world could go straight to hell.

Two days later, a hospital-style bed was delivered for Naomi's room. The beast arrived in an impressive, red and white ambulance. Two more men in white pants and jackets struggled to carry her into the house on a stretcher. They lifted her big body onto her new bed. A nurse positioned her and pulled the sheet and blanket up to her chin. Naomi stared at the ceiling and moaned. The nurse in a white uniform wiped dribble off the monster's toothless mouth. Naomi didn't appear to understand where she was or who was around her. The beast didn't scream out my name and demand to know where I was or what I was doing.

Nevertheless, "Where are you, Stupid!" still echoed through my head.

The nurse raised the bed's side rails to lock Naomi in. The beast looked like she was behind bars in a prison cell. Relief and happiness surged through me.

Sympathy showed on the nurse's face as she turned and spoke to me. She thought I felt sorry for Naomi and worried about her. The only thing that worried me was people thinking it was my fault and I belonged in a reform school.

"Mickey is your name, right dear?"

"Yes, ma'am."

"Naomi can't hear or see you. She doesn't know you're standing next to her." She placed her hand gently on my shoulder. "We hope she'll get better soon. We're all praying for her."

"Yes, ma'am."

She smiled at me. "You need to be brave and pray for her too, Mickey."

"Yes, ma'am." Jesus Christ. What a relief. Naomi really didn't know what was happening around her. The chances were much better that she wouldn't notice the money missing from her purse. The nurse's hand on my shoulder made me flinch, and I felt bad about that. I wasn't used to gentleness from humans. I couldn't stop from flinching whenever anyone moved their hand in my direction.

The next day, I was allowed to stand close to Naomi again. I was curious about what a person in a coma was like and exactly what they could see and do. Naomi still moaned and dribbled spit and stared at the ceiling. The beast couldn't raise her arms. But, with the side rail down, I didn't stand too close to her. She might recover all of a sudden, and erupt in a rage. It was really strange to be so close to Naomi and not see her eyes full of hate and rage directed at me. For the first time, I noticed her eyes were a dirty-brown color with red streaks through the whites. She smelled so awful I wanted to gag. I also hated the medicine smell of the room, but I didn't want my disgust to be too obvious and cause the nurse to feel bad.

One of the nurses hired to attend to Naomi was a neighbor who lived three blocks down Hamlin Avenue. Warm-hearted and embracing, Anna invited me to visit her home and her family. Despite my fear of people, I accepted.

The next evening, I ate dinner with her, her husband, and their two children, a boy and a girl who were both younger than me. I wasn't scared or intimidated by any of them. Since they weren't the perfect Dick and Jane family like I read about in the books at school, I didn't feel like a freak when I visited their house. They were hard-working Polish people. Anna was an excellent cook, and I was always hungry. Her family showed no reluctance to share their food with me. I was glad they didn't know the kind of family I came from. My supposed father would've called them dirty Pollocks and told racist jokes about them.

After dinner, we watched their television. Professional wrestling, at ten-o'clock on Wednesday night, was their favorite program. We ate buttered popcorn Anna popped on her stove as we cheered and booed the wrestlers. The father, who loved to laugh, was usually the rowdiest. He yelled encouragement to the good guys and booed Gorgeous George and the other villainous, big-star wrestlers. They dimmed the lights in their small living room for the best viewing. I loved to sit amidst those wonderful people in the glow of the small, black and white television screen. Nobody cared how late it was or how sleepy we all were. The whole family stayed up late to watch and cheer wrestling.

When I was isolated in my room at Naomi's, I listened to the neighbor's television through the door that separated us. I hadn't watched a real television screen since I lived with Rose and George five years ago. Now I couldn't watch enough. I didn't have to create the scenes in my mind using just the words and noises that blared from the speakers. I could actually see the pictures that went with all the sounds.

I lived so close to these kind people, yet they hadn't known of my existence until Naomi had her stroke. Naomi's stroke definitely changed my life for the better.

After visits with my friends, I walked home alone. In the dark, those three blocks seemed much longer. The hair on the back of my neck stood up straight and a cold chill coursed down my spine as I imagined any number of horrors popping out of shadowy recesses and dark doorways along my route. I constantly fought the urge to break into a panicky run. Despite all that, I visited those generous people as often as possible and stayed as late as they allowed me.

Chapter 32

During one of my trips to the corner market, I saw a sign that read: Newspaper Delivery Boys Wanted. I walked to the address listed and paced back and forth outside the two-story granite building until I worked up the courage to enter the front door and find my way to the proper desk.

"I'd like to deliver newspapers, sir," I blurted out.

The large, balding man, who shuffled papers and answered constantly ringing telephones, looked at me with surprise and doubt.

"You think you can be a delivery boy," he said in a gruff voice. "You're really small and skinny. How old are you, buster?"

"I'm twelve-years-old, sir, twelve and a half, really."

"Really?"

"Yes, sir. I am. I can do the job. When I was younger, I sold newspapers downtown with my two older brothers. I shined shoes, I dove for golf balls, and I collected deposit bottles. I know how to work, sir."

"What's your name?"

"Mickey Johnson, sir."

"Okay, kid." He said with a tiny smile. "We'll give you a shot at it."

Mr. Gruff assigned me to a route with forty-five customers. He handed me a receipt book with a list of the addresses I'd deliver to and the amount of money I should collect. He also gave me two over-the-shoulder canvas bags to carry my newspapers in.

"If you lose those bags, you have to pay for them. Understand, kid?"

"Yes, sir. I understand."

This was the first job I worked completely on my own that paid real money. I was excited to discover I was good at it. After I was perfect at delivering the daily newspaper, I found a weekly paper that needed delivery boys. A local edition nobody subscribed to, I placed a paper once a week at fifty people's front door and went by once a month to collect. I was paid half of what I could persuade people to pay me, and I didn't give one thought to being anything but totally honest about how much money I collected.

I climbed dark stairways, sometimes five and six stories high, and walked dim, smelly hallways to deliver those two different newspapers. For the weekly paper, I knocked on doors and asked people to pay for ten pages of mostly advertising few of them wanted. Some paid just to make me go away, and some shouted through their closed door, "I don't want that damn newspaper, kid. You'd better quit bothering me, or I'll call the cops on you."

I knocked at one intimidating door, where a burly man with a dirty T-shirt stretched over his huge belly ripped the door open, looked down at me and growled, "I told you I don't want that goddamn newspaper." He sized me up with gradually softening eyes. Suddenly, he turned around and yelled into his apartment, "Oh hell, you deal with this." He disappeared into his boiled-cabbage smelling cave, and a woman quickly replaced him at the door. Heavily wrinkled, wearing thick makeup, and sporting puffy, orange hair, she held a lit cigarette between her costume-jewelry decorated fingers. She smelled like she'd spilled a full bottle of perfume on herself. She didn't appear to be dangerous though.

"How old are you, darling?"

"I'm twelve, ma'am," I replied in my sweetest voice.

Her broad smile showed yellow, uneven, lipstick-smudged teeth. She searched through her bright-green, plastic purse.

"Here you are, dear." She paid me the full amount due plus a generous tip. As she patted my hand, her lipstick-stained cigarette bobbed between her trembling lips.

"You're such a pretty boy, dear," she mumbled.

"Thanks a lot, ma'am."

She pulled her cigarette from between her thin, old lips and exhaled a cloud of smoke into my face.

"Oh, you're welcome, honey. Any time, dear."

I fled before she could reach out, pinch my cheek, and ask me to tell her the sad story of my life.

I kept busy with my two paper routes and made good money. I emptied Naomi's coin purse, and nobody suspected me of being a thief. God knew about my stealing and every other sin I committed. I didn't want to cause him more pain, so I swore I wouldn't steal again, except from Naomi.

Had God decided to help me? While Naomi was in her coma, I was free. Until she recovered, there wouldn't be any scrubbing and waxing floors on my hands and knees or bending over a scrub board washing laundry by hand in the shadowy basement. There wouldn't be any more screaming and beatings. There wouldn't be any more forced solitude. If the monster never recovered, I wouldn't ever go back to school. I'd deliver newspapers for the rest of my life and eat all the hot dogs, potato chips, cupcakes, and ice cream bars I wanted. Never again would anyone tell me what to do.

I did need to avoid the bullies who roamed everywhere, and the creepy men who stalked the streets and parks looking for solitary young boys. And I needed to keep a close watch on my hard-earned money.

I stayed away from the house most of the time, and Emil didn't appear to notice or care. I heard the nurses in Naomi's room and caught sight of the activity in that stinking place through the open door. The few times I ventured in, she lay on her back in her hospital bed with her blank stare and barely audible moans. Saliva dribbled onto her chin and covers. Day after day, she lay there. She was the prisoner, while I ran the streets of Chicago. I was free. Thank you, Jesus Christ, for rescuing me.

One day, I walked in while the nurse was bathing her. Naomi's bottom half was naked, and I saw her dark hairy thing with wrinkled flaps that hung down. Before, I'd only seen hairless young girls with a crack barely exposed by the swell of that place, and I'd seen a couple of pictures of naked women with lots of hair there. This was my first time to see a real one close-up. Damn. It was scary.

At times they propped Naomi up on her side with her face to the wall, and I saw only the back of her. Her false teeth sat in a glass of water on her dresser, unused and soaking, waiting until God restored her to a normal life. She only ate soft food now, and somebody needed to spoon her meals into her mouth. The stuff they fed her looked exactly like the gruel she'd forced me to eat every morning. That yellow, mealy stuff always dribbled out of her mouth, over her lower lip and down her chin, and collected on the towel that covered her neck and the top of her nightgown. I wondered if the monster could really taste that awful stuff. I hoped she could. Ha!

I couldn't forget her making me clean her teeth.

"Mickey! Have you finished cleaning my teeth yet?"

"Yes, ma'am, I have."

"Bring them to me now!"

"Yes, ma'am."

"You better have done a perfect job on them!"

"I did."

Naomi didn't wear her false teeth all the time, so they sat in a glass of water to soak. Food residue broke free and floated around turning the water murky. My job was to change the water and clean her teeth using a small brush and baking soda. After I'd brushed her teeth clean and sparkly, she inspected them closely. With her teeth out, Naomi's face sunk and showed even more wrinkles than usual, and pale white gums when she opened her big mouth. She looked so comical when she wasn't wearing her false teeth. I wanted to laugh at her. Of course, she'd kill me if I did.

On another day, I was alone in the room with the beast. I used one of her fancy forks I took from the dining room to test her alertness by lifting her covers and jabbing the sharp points into her fat side. Her body flinched, but she remained wordless and helpless, staring at the ceiling. A few specks of blood showed from the wound I inflicted. I made a second stab just to be sure. The tremor that coursed through her body both fascinated and disgusted me. I did feel a tiny bit guilty about stabbing her, but I had to be sure she still didn't know what was happening around her. My biggest fear in life was she'd wake up and discover all the freedom I'd enjoyed while she was in her coma and she'd kill me.

The cleaning woman, who came to the house once a week, didn't do as thorough a job as I had, but no one noticed or seemed to care. Naomi would've blown her top.

Chapter 33

Naomi died.

I was sitting at the dining room table when the doctor left, and the nurse approached me. I flinched when she put her hand on my shoulder, but it was just my expecting-to-be-hit habit. Her touch was gentle, and she smelled like a freshly cut rose.

"Your foster mother is with God now," she said in a soft voice.

"She's not my foster mother, ma'am. My real mother left me with her a few years ago. I'm just living here until Mom comes back for me."

"I'm sorry, Mickey."

Damn. She knew my name. "Naomi is really dead, nurse?"

"Yes. She passed away peacefully."

Tears forced their way into my eyes. I didn't understand why the hell I was crying.

The nurse looked at me with sympathy. "How old are you, Mickey?" she asked.

"I'm twelve and a half, ma-am." I sat up taller and wiped away my stupid tears.

"Your mother left you here when you were nine years old?"

"Yes, ma'am. But she said she'd come back for me as soon as she could."

I really liked this pretty nurse. I wished I could go live with her, but teary-eyed Emil followed her out the front door when she left. I guessed they needed to talk. Naomi and I were alone inside the house, and I was really spooked. I didn't believe the danger was gone, so I took one of the silver forks from her fancy dining room buffet, worked up my courage and entered her room. I looked at Naomi's supposedly dead body lying in the hospital bed. Her eyes were closed, so the lifeless stare of her coma was gone. Her moaning was silenced, the flow of dribble from her mouth stopped, and there wasn't any raspy breathing.

Emil hadn't come back inside, so I edged closer to Naomi. I lifted her cover, and I jabbed the fork into her fat side. There wasn't any movement of her body at all. There wasn't a moan of pain from the penetration of the fork tines. There wasn't a spurt of blood from the wound. She looked dead and reacted as if she were dead. I was never around a corpse before, and I still wasn't absolutely sure the creature was done with living. Only time would tell. I still didn't feel safe standing near her. Jesus Christ rose from the dead and went up to heaven, and I worried evil people, like Naomi, could rise from the dead and continue being brutal monsters on the earth.

Somewhat relieved, I left her room. I was glad she wasn't stomping around the house, and her screechy voice wasn't attacking my ears. I still didn't understand why I'd cried about her being dead.

They took Naomi's body away in a big, shiny undertaker's limousine. By the next morning, she was up front and center stage on display at a funeral home. They'd squeezed her big, fat body into an elaborately-carved, dark-wood casket lined with thick, white satin. Her big head rested on a lace-edged, white satin pillow. The pillow looked much softer than she deserved. Flowers and somber music surrounded her. Paintings of Bible scenes hung on the wall behind her. Jesus Christ himself looked down at her with an expression of love. Didn't he know how evil she'd been?

Emil let me wear some of his good clothes for the viewing, service, and burial. I did a lot of rollups on the pant legs and shirt sleeves. The stupid tie hung down to my crotch, so I had to hold it aside when I took a piss. I stuffed newspaper in the toes of the shoes he let me borrow. His man shoes were still a better fit than the oversized clodhoppers Naomi had forced me to stagger about in.

It was difficult to breathe in the chapel of the funeral home. The many flower arrangements and her fancy casket gave off a thick smell that overloaded the air. Perfume smells to hide the death smell of Naomi poured out of her coffin. The old people who came to see her dead body wore lots of cologne to hide their old people smells.

I could walk by the monster's casket as many times as I wanted. I walked up and looked at her in her casket, again and again, to be sure she was still in there and was still dead. She looked more womanly in her fancy coffin than she ever had in life. Her hair was neatly permed, and well-applied makeup hid some of her ugliness. She wore a fine, black dress, and her brutish hands were neatly manicured and folded on her chest. Her big diamond ring was sparkling clean. They removed all traces of my blood from the ring that cut into my flesh when she hit me. There was almost a smile on Naomi's face, something I hadn't ever seen directed at me during my years as her slave. Somehow, they hid her terrible meanness. If she was floating around invisible, looking down at this scene, what would she think of herself? All this funeral stuff must have cost a lot of money. That would piss her off! Hoarding money had been the only joy of her life.

I was an important family member and had a front-row seat reserved especially for me. I didn't mind spending most of my day sitting there. I felt safer knowing the beast still lay dead and motionless in her fancy casket. Many of the old women who walked by to view Naomi acted like they were really sad she was dead. Some cried. Some said how lovely she looked, and what a lovely dress she wore, and what lovely flowers filled the room, and what a lovely casket she had, and what a lovely funeral hers was. The husbands gripped their hats in front of them and looked at embalmed Naomi like they didn't have any idea who the hell she was. People wearing their finest dark dresses and dark suits stopped by to comfort me. Jewelry jangled freely from the women mourners.

"You poor child," people whispered close to my ear.

Old women patted me on my head or my cheek with their gloved hands. Old men squeezed my shoulder with their big hands.

"Naomi was so kind to him. Naomi was so generous to have provided him with a loving home," they commented among themselves.

"That poor little boy must be so sad she died."

"His own mother didn't want him."

"How could a mother give away her own child?"

"That sweet, blond-haired boy really is an orphan now."

"What's going to happen to him?" a voice whispered loudly.

Damn! I hadn't thought about that. What was going to happen to me?

Emil and I were the last to leave the chapel. We stood next to the casket as the mortician struggled to remove Naomi's diamond ring from her thick finger. The ring finally popped free, and he handed it to tearful, grieving Emil. The man pulled the casket lid down and sealed it shut.

Jesus Christ, I thought. It must be scary dark inside that casket with the lid shut.

I listened closely for Naomi to scream in terror, but the monster remained silent.

Emil and I rode in a large, black limousine from the funeral home to the cemetery. I felt more important than I ever had in my life. It was just Emil and me in that fine automobile following the hearse that carried Naomi's dead body. Trailing behind us was a long line of cars with funeral signs on their dashboards. I couldn't believe there were so many mourners for Naomi. I couldn't understand why Naomi had been such a popular person.

The cemetery was a grassy, tree-lined park crowded with small to massive gravestones and statues. Corpses of the rich rested in elaborate marble buildings. Somber visitors placed fresh flowers on old graves. Bouquets, just starting to wilt, sagged against shiny, new headstones.

Our mourning party stood around a freshly dug, six-foot-deep hole with Naomi's casket suspended over it. Prayers were said to help Naomi's soul find its way to heaven. If Naomi was going to heaven, would she be waiting there to brutalize me again? I couldn't believe she'd fooled God. If anyone belonged in hell, she did.

After prayers were said, and tears were shed, the flower-draped casket was lowered into the hole until it rested at the bottom. Two men shoveled fresh earth onto it. Most of the people, talking quietly among themselves, wandered away. Emil and I stayed behind. He stayed out of respect, I guess. I wanted to be sure they got every speck of that black, wormy earth on top of the monster and her casket. I prayed she wouldn't ever escape from her grave.

Afterwards, the funeral party gathered at Emil's boss's fine, city house. Loud talk, laughter, and smiles quickly replaced the grief. Mourners feasted from a long table covered with platters, plates, and serving bowls heaped with ham, turkey, roast beef, cheese, breads, salads, and dozens of desserts. The sad funeral had turned into a festive party. I was finished with all the mourning crap, and most of the people ignored me. I ate until my stomach was stretched to its fullest. I remembered my brothers and wished they could see me now. They'd be so jealous of me because I was an important person at a fancy funeral, and I shared food with rich people.

Chapter 34

It was a huge relief that Naomi was dead, buried deep in the ground and hopefully gone from the world forever. I still needed to move carefully through the world and make sure nobody else tried to enslave me.

Grieving Emil went back to work. He didn't seem concerned about what I did, or how I spent my time. I had my own key to the house and kept busy with my paper routes. I spent my money on sodas, cupcakes, candy bars, comic books, and movie admissions. After Naomi had suffered her stroke, I readapted to navigating the streets of Chicago like I had with my two older brothers, several years ago. It was tougher being alone, but, if the stray dogs and wild alley cats could survive, so could I. I didn't trust anybody, and was always ready to run for safety. I continued to avoid bullies and perverts looking for solitary, young boys.

I thought about Mom. Was Mom alive somewhere and living in a huge mansion? Was she rich with all the pretty possessions she always wanted? Did she think about me? I doubted it. She never intended to come back and rescue me from the monster, Naomi. Damn her to hell. Would I ever see her again? Did I even want to?

I couldn't worry about that kind of baby stuff anymore. I was on my own in the world and stuck with my new life of freedom.

Following Naomi's death and burial, I wondered what Emil's intentions were regarding my future. Was he thinking about my three and a half years of slavery to his awful wife? It was also possible he hadn't given one moment's thought to my welfare. Had his childhood been so bad he thought the way Naomi brutalized me was the way all kids were treated. He wasn't a cruel person. He never yelled at me or hit me or went out of his way to touch me.

Emil invited me to go on an outing with him. His wanting to spend time with me was a huge surprise. I willingly accepted his offer.

On a Saturday morning, after I delivered my newspapers, Emil and I drove to downtown Chicago and the famous lakefront parks. He was a good driver, and I enjoyed the sights along our route. I continued to keep a sharp eye out for any sight of Mom or my brothers.

First, we visited the Field Museum of Natural History in Grant Park. A huge Tyrannosaurus Rex skeleton towered over us as we entered the massive granite building. I was glad I hadn't lived when that killer dinosaur was around. He'd have run me down, and with one quick gulp, I'd be down his throat and into his stomach.

The large Wooly Mammoths impressed me with their dense, hairy coats and long curved tusks. I wouldn't want to hunt one of those Stone Age elephants armed with only a spear.

A Stone Age family display of two parents and an eight-year-old boy made me envious. Here was a family that looked like they cared about each other. The father would courageously fight off wild beasts to protect his wife and son. He wouldn't walk away and abandon his family like my bully of a father had.

On this sunny, wind-free summer day, Lake Michigan was a calm, sparkling blue. Emil bought hot dogs and sodas from a vendor cart near Buckingham Fountain for our lunch. We sat on the concrete steps that circled the elaborate fountain to eat. Flocks of pigeons surrounded us and brazenly approached as we ate our hot dogs heaped with mustard, relish, and onions.

Our next stop was nearby Shedd Aquarium with its huge fish tank populated with big sharks, stingrays, and sea bass. Hundreds of other fish, small and large, swam close to the thick glass and looked me right in the eye. The hammerhead shark was my favorite. His entire body whipped from side to side as he sped around looking for prey. I wouldn't want to encounter him after my warship had been sunk by a torpedo and I was a thrashing sailor adrift on the high seas.

On these weekend excursions, Emil was fun to be around. Maybe this was how life would be with a decent father who cared what happened to me. Emil wasn't really what I'd want in a father, but he was a friend to me on these outings. His friendliness did confuse me though. For the last few years, Emil had watched how cruelly Naomi had treated me, and he never offered me one bit of help or sympathy.

Hell. It must be the way most people are. They pretended they cared about you one minute and the next minute, they ignored your existence. If you were an unwanted kid, nobody offered to help you. Unwanted kids were too much bother for anyone to care about them. Unwanted kids were left to survive on their own in the world.

Emil and I returned to Grant Park on Sunday to visit the Art Institute. The famous paintings gave me a view into a different world. I struggled to comprehend how some people had the skill to create such vivid, lifelike pictures on a piece of canvas. My own efforts to draw and paint were limited to stick figures and muddy blotches of color. I liked seeing the beautiful art, even though it made me feel low on the scale of human achievement and worth.

For lunch, we had hot dogs again, a meal I'd happily consume daily for the rest of my life. Afterwards, we walked among the luxurious boats moored at the Chicago Yacht Club. I imagined being rich someday and living on my own big yacht. If I had lots of money, I might adopt some poor, unwanted kids and let them live on the boat with me. For now, though, I wanted to go out on the lake aboard one of the biggest and fastest boats. I wanted to speed across the water and find a sunny, isolated island with a warm, sandy beach. There might be an abandoned dog on the island I'd become best friends with, and together we'd eat fish and bananas, and I wouldn't ever again fear the bullies of the world.

The next Saturday, after I'd delivered my newspapers, Emil and I spent the day at the Lincoln Zoo. I vaguely remembered being there when I was young. That memory brought my mother and my brothers back into my thoughts, and I didn't want to think about them, because I'd start bawling like a baby. I wanted to believe nobody mattered to me anymore. Still, the zoo was a place I never got bored with. I enjoyed visiting every one of the animals, except the red-assed, screeching monkeys. We bought bags of peanuts and threw some to the sad-faced elephants. The elephants were really big, but they didn't have much room to run, and there wasn't any grass or trees for them to enjoy. They weren't like the crazed, trumpeting movie elephants that stampeded through native villages crushing people to death.

The smell of the fish, the zoo sold visitors to feed the seals, brought back memories of fishing off the piers with Tommy and Ben, and the fun we had together. I wondered if I'd ever see any of my brothers again.

I still didn't understand why Emil acted so generous and paid for all these fun trips. I was a kid nobody wanted, and I wasn't doing slave work at his house anymore. There wasn't any reason for him to treat me decently.

The following weekend, Emil and I went to Jackson Park, which was further south along the lakefront. Our timing was perfect. A German U-boat, captured by brave American sailors during World War Two, was being moved in for display at the Museum of Science and Industry. We crowded close to the curb, and the sub towered over us as truck-trailers slowly hauled it down Leif Erickson Drive. I imagined the submarine, full of brave sailors, speeding along deep underwater, ready for combat. Then the sub rose up swiftly, its periscope broke through the choppy seas, and it leveled off close to the surface.

"Fire one!"

"Fire Two!"

Torpedoes raced towards a helpless American merchant ship. There were thunderous explosions and towers of fire as the torpedoes hit their easy target. Frightened seamen jumped overboard into the flaming ocean.

An angry American destroyer raced to the attack.

"Dive, dive," shouted the Krauts. "Dive!"

Depth charges launched from the speeding sub-killer like large boulders flung from a catapult. Those deadly containers made a big splash, sank below the surface creating a mass of bubbles and exploded into a large circle of underwater flames. The submarine shuddered from bow to stern. Water flooded through a hole in the sub's hull and trapped the panicked German sailors inside. The crippled U-boat plummeted to the depths of the ocean. The enemy crew, many who were young boys, all drowned. I was awed and horrified by that scene in the theater newsreels and war movies.

Inside the Museum, we rode a noisy, bone-jarring, little train through a coal mine that was supposed to be just like the real thing. With Naomi dead and buried, I didn't have to descend into a shadowy basement to shovel coal and breathe its dust. Emil now did the furnace maintenance and kept the stoker full. Maybe he thought Naomi had done all the dirty jobs around the house. He didn't appear to know how to boss around and make use of a child slave.

We climbed aboard and walked through full-sized railroad cars at the railroad display. Those cars reminded me of the train trips I took with my mother and my brothers when we were fleeing from angry Dad, or after our family had been abandoned by Dad.

Emil admired the antique automobiles that were a part of his history. He finally talked with a little excitement in his voice.

High above us, wires suspended historic, full-size airplanes from the ceiling. We went up to the next floor and strolled the walkway next to the aircraft. These very planes fought dogfights and flew bombing raids against the Japs and Krauts during World War Two.

I really enjoyed all the stuff Emil and I were doing and seeing. After so much time confined to my room, I was out in the world again. I'd missed so much of life during the last few years while I was a slave to Naomi. I had a lot of catching up to do.

The flurry of fun trips ended. The father and son weekend excursions stopped dead cold, and Emil went back to ignoring me. He didn't have anything to say to me. I guessed we'd done all the fun stuff he wanted to do. He fooled me into believing he wanted to spend time with me and had been thinking about keeping me as his kid. I wanted to kick myself for being stupid enough to fall into that trap again. Damn all people.

Chapter 35

Naomi was dead, and Emil didn't care what I did. I was twelve-years-old, totally alone in the world, and on my own to survive. I was suspicious of everything and everyone.

Still figuring out my new world of freedom, I often visited nearby Garfield Park. Families with their treasured children fed the swans, ducks, pigeons, and squirrels that crowded the lakeshore and the spacious, grass lawns. Couples-in-love sat close together on benches and embraced so tightly they looked like one fat person. Couples cuddled on blankets spread over the soft grass, or clumsily rowed rental-rowboats on the lake while they stared stupidly into each other's eyes. Cheerful-people voices echoed off the water and throughout the wide-spreading, leafy trees. Bright-eyed robins hopped about hunting for worms. Shiny-black crows swooped up into the trees and down to the lawns and cawed noisily. The numerous jays scolded everyone with their screechy voices.

Solitary men, old and young, fat and thin, ugly and handsome, wandered the park. Too many of them looked at me. A few tried to talk to me. I didn't trust any of them. I did my best to avoid those creepy, scary strangers.

I needed to take a leak, so I reluctantly went into the public men's restroom. The drab inside consisted of two toilet stalls with battered doors, three rusty sinks with dirty mirrors above them, a pull-down cloth-towel machine and a single, yellowed-white ceramic trough urinal about ten feet long. The smell of stale piss filled the air.

A man stood at the end of the trough holding his thing, but not pissing. I edged up to the urinal, unzipped my fly, pulled it out and forced my yellow stream to start. The man turned to look at me. He waggled his thing. I didn't have a lot to waggle, and I didn't want to see his damn thing.

I hated these kinds of places to relieve myself. If I had a foot-long one and could stand a foot back to urinate, I wouldn't have to stand in the yellow puddles of piss on the floor in front of the urinals.

A few inches from my eyes, a crude drawing on the wall showed a man on his knees with a standing man's thing in his mouth. Another drawing showed a naked man bent over at his waist with another man's long, fat thing shoved against the cheeks of his ass. It looked like some of it was actually inside the man's asshole. I finished pissing, and in a hurry to get out of there, I hadn't shaken it enough, and urine dribbled down my leg. The filthy mirrors above the sinks reflected the image of the man standing at the trough still shaking his thing.

As I walked to the exit door, another man came in. He paused and looked me over. He was blocking my escape, but I dodged past him and rushed out of there.

"Hello, son." echoed after me.

The next week I was back in the park and needed to use the public toilets again. Another creepy looking man stood at the trough, so I went into a stall. There was piss all over the filthy toilet seat and floor. A hole had been gouged through the metal partition that separated the two stalls. A scratchy drawing of hair around the hole made it look like a girl's thing. Crudely printed instructions on the wall above the toilet said: *Call this phone number for a good blow job.*

I heard someone else enter the men's room. Footsteps echoed across the white, tile floor, and paused in front of my stall. I froze. I heard him breathing and saw his fine gentleman shoes under the stall door. I listened as his body shifted about. Please, don't say anything to me. He walked on to the trough urinal.

Two men now shared the trough and murmured to each other. I rushed out of the stinking stall and restroom as fast as I could without breaking into a panicky run.

I sat on a nearby park bench to catch my breath and tried to be invisible. Trough man number-two showed up and sat down at the end of my bench. I knew it was him because of his shoes. My Chicago shoeshine boy instincts were still sharp. The creep gave me a sideways look. I didn't want to leave and appear scared. Maybe he didn't want anything from me. He left without saying a word. I was safe. Another man walked towards my bench. He sat down too close to me.

"How are you doing, son?"

I wasn't his son. Why do they always say that?

Pale faced, with thin lips and milky green eyes, he wore a dark brown suit with a white shirt and plain brown tie.

"My name is Eric."

"Yes, sir." Jesus. I didn't want to know his name. I didn't want to talk to him at all, but it wasn't easy for me to be rude to grownups.

"How old are you, son?"

"I'm twelve, sir."

"Twelve. You look younger."

"I'm actually twelve and a half, sir."

"Do you live nearby?"

"Down Hamlin Avenue." I thumbed in that direction.

"How come you're always alone in the park?"

"Just—because."

"You're not the talkative type, are you?"

"No, sir." This guy really gave me the creeps.

"Have you eaten dinner yet, son?"

"No, sir."

"Are you hungry?"

"Not really, sir."

"Would you like to go to dinner with me?"

"I don't think so." I really needed to get away from this guy.

"I'm going to the diner at the corner for dinner. They serve really good cheeseburgers and wonderful milkshakes there."

"I better not."

"It's just a friendly dinner. What did you say your name was?"

"Mickey," I muttered.

I hated that he had so much pleading in his voice and manner. I was low on money, and I was hungry. I hated going back to my room to be alone, and he seemed pretty harmless.

He smiled at me again. I didn't like his smile. Not many grownups had a good smile.

"Well," Eric said. "Would you like a cheeseburger and a milkshake, Mickey? I'll buy."

"I guess so." After I thought about it, I was sure I could easily escape from him if I needed to.

"Let's go now, Mickey, before the restaurant gets crowded."

"Okay."

As we stood up and started for the diner, he put his hand on my shoulder. I flinched and moved away from him. I hated when anyone touched me. His expression said I hurt his feelings. I didn't want to hurt anyone's feelings.

"I'm sorry, but I have to go home, sir." I walked away from him as fast as I could without breaking into a run.

"Mickey!" I hated the sound of his pleading voice calling out to me.

I avoided the park for a while, but I still wandered Chicago's scary streets. Wherever I went by myself, the men always lurked nearby. It was worse in some places than others. When I went to a sparsely attended movie, I sat in the center of the dark theatre, as far away from other patrons as possible. But the men closed in on me like long-clawed crabs scuttling across a beach to feast on a crippled bird.

A body moved across the row of seats behind me. The body sat down in the seat directly behind me. The body movement, the clearing of the throat, the heavy breathing and the suffocating lust sent tremors of revulsion through my body. I wanted to scream, "LEAVE ME ALONE!"

When I wandered about the city, I constantly reminded myself to always be careful. Don't trust anyone. Avoid eye contact. Always appear angry and dangerous. My problem was I looked even younger than my twelve years. I was too frail; my hair was too blond, and my eyes were too blue. Everything about me made me look like a helpless, little kid. Even though I was dressed like a low-down street urchin in my oversized old-man clothes, no matter how much I tried, I couldn't look dangerous. I always looked like a frightened, little sissy who needed his mommy.

Chapter 36

Emil's and my peaceful coexistence ended. He brought plump, big-breasted Priscilla to the house. She had fire-red hair and lots of freckles; her lips were full, her large eyes a bright green, and her nose too small for her broad face. Much younger than Emil, she never wore makeup, dressed like a plain, country person and spoke loudly with a heavy southern accent.

I was alone with her in the kitchen and thought maybe she and I could be friends.

"Are you from Chicago?" I asked her.

"No. I'm from West Virginia, Mickey," she said proudly.

"My mother was born in Georgia," I replied. "She was born in an Army tent. My grandfather was a soldier in the American army."

"You really don't have any idea where your mother is, do you, Mickey?"

"No, I don't."

"She isn't much of a mother to you, is she, Mickey?"

"She was always wonderful to me when I lived with her. She always said she loved me. My father abandoned us, and Mom didn't have enough money to take care of me and all my brothers."

"If she left you here with strangers, she didn't love you very much."

"She said she loved me a lot."

"She really said she loved you?"

"I know she loved me."

Priscilla shook her head and let out a big sigh. She looked at me like she couldn't believe how stupid I was. Her talking bad about Mom ended my wanting to be friends. She really couldn't stand the sight of me and didn't want me around her and Emil. She didn't want me around the house at all. A war erupted between us, and I didn't have a chance in hell against a person as tricky as her. After the conversation about my mother, she didn't speak directly to me but complained about me to Emil all the time. The little I overheard was a pack of dirty lies.

I surprised Emil and her one day by walking into the apartment while they were in the bedroom. There was a big commotion like Emil and she getting dressed in a hurry. They rushed out to the parlor. Priscilla confronted me with a red-faced, killer look. Sweaty and also red-faced, Emil stood meekly next to her. He looked guilty of the worst sin ever committed by a human.

"You sneak around the house like a dirty thief, Mickey!" She sounded just like a witch from the movies.

She was right about me being a sneak. I wasn't a thief anymore, but I'd become an expert sneak and a sharp-eared eavesdropper. I wanted to know what people were thinking and saying about me, and I was in big trouble with her.

"You need to find his mother, Emil," Priscilla nagged at him. "He's going to be a big problem for us."

"I won't be a bother," I pleaded to Emil. "I promise."

My words were useless. Emil didn't listen to me at all. Priscilla would put her arm across his shoulders and touch his ear with the tips of her fingers, and his face would flush. She'd give me a you-don't-have-a-fucking-chance-against-me-kid look. I guessed she was a slut, and Emil was sticking his old penis into her.

It was apparent Priscilla wanted me out of the house and out of her life, as soon as possible. Margaret, the polio-crippled neighbor who was one of my few friends, called Priscilla a hick, hillbilly, redneck, inbred, cracker and ridge runner.

"She probably eats squirrels and such," Margaret continued. "She's roadkill-eating, southern white trash."

Jesus Christ. Margaret was tougher than I'd imagined. She might hit Priscilla over the head with her crutch and kill her.

Priscilla moved into the house and into Emil's room. Soon after, her son showed up. Six-foot-tall and at least two-hundred-fifty pounds of fat, he had the same fire-red hair as Priscilla and a pimply face. He looked at me like I was a small animal he'd enjoy torturing to death.

Soon after his arrival, he trapped me in the vestibule as I was leaving the house.

"So, you're the orphan." He sneered down at me.

"I'm not an orphan. My mother is alive, and she's rich, and she's waiting for me to come back home to her."

"You're so full of shit, kid."

I tried to get past him, but he blocked my escape. He was scary big and smelled like he hadn't taken a bath for weeks. He bumped against me with his big, stinking body.

"You better listen to me, orphan. That room you're living in is supposed to be mine."

"Sorry."

"Sorry, shit. You'd better find someplace else to live."

I ducked under his arm and hurried out the front door. I would never have another peaceful night's rest as long as I lived in this house with Priscilla and her bully boy. The room he claimed was my prison cell for nearly four years, but it was still the only place I had to sleep. With Priscilla and Curtis as enemies, my freedom was a scary illusion.

I was really in trouble. There was no place for me to go. Living with Emil was all I had, and he didn't want me around. What the hell was I supposed to do? Damn the whole stinking world.

"I need to talk to you, Mickey," Emil said.

Oh, no. Something really terrible is about to happen.

"We're going to drive to St. Charles and visit one of your brothers."

"I'll see one of my brothers! Are you sure? Which one?"

"Your younger brother, Steve."

"Really! I get to see Steve. I hardly remember him. What about Tommy and Ben? Do you know where they are?"

"Doris says she has information about Tommy and Ben."

"Wow! My brothers." I'd given up all hope of ever seeing any of them again.

Chapter 37

Emil and I set out for Saint Charles. I was going to have a reunion with my younger brother, Steve. Apprehension attacked me in waves as we covered mile after mile on roads I barely remembered. Most vivid in my mind was the tears and confusion on five-year-old Steve's face when Mom, Ben and I walked out and left him behind with Doris. It had been such a sad day. Doris picked Steve rather than me or Ben. Jesus Christ. At least Rose and George had taken me in for a year and acted like I was their kid and even wanted to adopt me. I made my terrible decision to go back home with my mother when she visited Christmas day. Now, I was twelve-years-old, and nobody in the world wanted to own me as their kid.

When we pulled up in front of her house, nothing was as big or grand as I remembered. Doris looked older and heavier than I expected. She smiled and invited us inside. I felt extreme excitement and terrible anxiety.

Then I saw him, my younger brother Steve wearing a black suit, white shirt, tie, and black-framed eyeglasses. He looked at Emil and me shyly. I couldn't believe one of my brothers wore a suit. I remembered Mike, the fat kid, who was now officially Steve's younger brother. He was taller and fatter and still hid behind Steve.

"Yes, I remember Mickey." Doris placed her hand on my shoulder. I flinched, but she kept her hand there. "It's good to see you again, Mickey."

She spoke to Emil. "I felt so terrible I couldn't offer Mickey and Ben a home too. I never understood Virginia. She left her three sons overnight with me so I could choose which one I wanted to keep. How could a mother give her own children away to strangers?"

I didn't like her criticism of Mom.

Steve and I were sent to the backyard so Emil and Doris could talk. Mike followed us, but he kept his distance from me like he thought I was some dangerous Chicago thug. Steve sat on a swing suspended from a tree. I tried to converse. I was twelve and Steve was ten. We'd been as close as pups in a litter when we were young brothers living together in the slums of Chicago, but we hadn't seen each other for a long, five years.

"I remember climbing this tree," I said. "Ben and I climbed up this tree really fast. Ben went the highest."

"I don't remember that," Steve said. "Who's Ben?"

"Ben's one of our older brothers, Steve." Jesus Christ! How could Steve have forgotten Ben? I remembered lots of stuff from when I was five. Steve didn't even remember his own brother.

"Do you remember our oldest brother Tommy?"

"No."

"Do you remember me?"

"No. I'm sorry. I don't remember any of that stuff."

I wanted to burst into tears, but there wasn't any way I'd be a crybaby in front of my little brother.

"This tree is a great climbing tree." I looked up into the tree. I was choking on my words. "You tried to climb this tree, Steve. You jumped up, but you couldn't reach the lowest branch. You were a little runt back then."

"I don't remember that. Mike and I don't climb trees much."

"You don't climb trees?"

"My mom, Doris worries. She thinks Mike or I will fall and get hurt."

"Hell, Steve. Back in Chicago, we gang of brothers used to do lots of stuff way more dangerous than climbing a tree."

Steve had called Doris, "Mom." That really hurt me. When we were with our real family, we had the same mother, our real mother.

"I don't remember that. Doris doesn't allow us to swear either."

"Well, it was damn dangerous on the streets of Chicago." Hell! I felt like I'd lost a brother, not found one. Things that were important to me didn't seem to matter to Steve. He wasn't as excited to see me as I was to see him.

As we walked around the yard, Steve showed me some of his secret hiding places. He talked about his favorite games and toys. Mike followed us, but he didn't say anything that mattered. He did mumble some stupid, little-kid stuff.

"I have a couple of paper routes," I bragged. "I go to the movies all the time. I buy comic books, hamburgers, and hot dogs. I buy Hostess snowballs, Twinkies, and cupcakes. I eat Snickers candy bars and drink bottles of orange and chocolate soda. I eat whatever I want, whenever I want. I go wherever I want to go and stay out as late as I want."

They shook their heads in amazement as I rattled on. So what if I exaggerated a little bit. They stared at me like I was a genuine hoodlum.

"That stuff sounds better than what we do," Steve said.

"Sounds good to me too," Mike repeated. He sounded like one of those stupid parrots that mimicked everything people said.

Before we left to go back to Chicago, Doris had Steve play the piano for us. Emil sat quietly and listened. I found sitting still difficult, especially for boring piano music. I guess Steve played okay, but I couldn't believe my younger brother sat there obediently, wearing a suit, and playing a piano.

Steve and I didn't touch each other during the visit. No wrestling. No punching. Not even bumping into each other. Steve waved goodbye to us when we left. As Emil and I drove away, I felt a terrible emptiness inside of me. Would I ever see my younger brother again? Why the hell couldn't we be together like brothers are supposed to be?

Steve had it made. He hadn't been a slave and a prisoner like I had. He hadn't been screamed at and beaten every day. He wore decent clothes and ate lots of good food and lived with people who cared about him. I'd almost been adopted by Doris. If only I'd behaved better when Ben, Steve and I visited Doris five years ago, she might have picked me. I really screwed up.

On the drive back to Chicago, Emil told me what he learned from Doris. After she abandoned me at Naomi's, Mom was left with the last two of her five sons. Tommy got into serious trouble, and Mom had to go to court with him. She told the judge she couldn't deal with him anymore and agreed with the judge he should be sent to Boys Town, in Omaha, Nebraska.

He arrived at that famous reform school when he was twelve-years and two-months-old. He ran away five times during his first nine months there. They didn't have barbwire fences and armed guards, so how did they expect to keep him from running? After a while, they gave up on him. Nobody knew where he was now. Tommy was always the toughest and wildest of us five brothers.

Once Tommy went to Boys Town, Mom was left with just Ben. Damn Ben! He'd always wanted her all to himself.

They stayed at her mother's house in Saint Louis while Mom worked as a waitress. She found a man who wanted her, but the jerk didn't want ten-year-old Ben around. Mom left Ben at a St. Louis orphanage. She and that man hit the road looking for adventure.

I figure Mom lied to Ben, told him she loved him, and she'd be back soon to reclaim him, and they'd be together forever, just like she'd lied to me. But she walked away from him and disappeared exactly like she'd done to me. Damn.

I'm sure Ben was a sucker like I'd been and believed Mom would come back like she'd promised. At least Ben had the other orphans for company. He was probably one of the toughest kids living there, and he knew how to take advantage of that. He'd practiced plenty on me.

I would've been happier at an orphanage than being Naomi's slave. If I had clothes and shoes that fit me, I would've been tougher than most of the other orphans.

Ben spent two years at the orphanage. He regularly lined up for viewing by people looking for a kid. But, a ten to twelve-year-old boy with a tough street-look, didn't have any hope for a decent home or adoption by a loving family.

Ben was taken in by a farm couple for a short while. Their own son had gone off to fight in Korea, and they needed help on their farm. Eventually, they returned Ben to the orphanage because he wasn't strong enough or tough enough for the grueling farm work, and he didn't like the isolation of living out in the country.

Finally, one visitor to the orphanage, an airline pilot, who'd been an orphan himself, befriended Ben and decided to help him.

During my terrible life with Naomi, I imagined my brothers still lived happily with our mother in Chicago. I pictured them having a great time on the city streets. But that wasn't the reality.

"The airline pilot was persistent," Emil continued. "He found out your mother was remarried and living in Colorado. He contacted her and told her to take Ben back, or he'd inform the authorities. That was more than a year ago."

"Ben's living with our mother?"

"That's right. On his twelfth birthday, he boarded a train bound for Greeley Colorado," Emil said. "Your brother, Ben, is back with your mother."

The rest of the drive back to Chicago rushed by in a blur. My mind was twisted by jealousy and hate. Ben was back with Mom! Damn, him! Why did Ben get to be back with her and I didn't? Did she love him that much more than she ever loved me? Didn't she love me at all?

I dreamed about Mom that night.

Mom and I were in bed together. She hugged me and held me close to her body. All of a sudden, Ben was at the side of the bed standing over us. He screamed, "Get away from my mother, Mickey!" He grabbed me by my hair and pulled me away from her. I fell onto the floor. He kicked me viciously on my spine, and I was paralyzed. I lay helpless on the floor. Ben crawled into the bed and lay next to Mom. She hugged him and held him close to her body. He turned to me and gave me his smuggest "I'm the winner" look.

"Stay away from my mother, Mickey!"

I woke up on the floor of my room, achy and sweaty. I had a boner. I reluctantly climbed back into bed. I was afraid to go back to sleep. I didn't want the dream to continue.

I grabbed my pillow and humped it until my penis stung. I always felt terribly depressed after I did that awful thing. I hated myself, but it was still the best feeling I had in my stupid life.

I tried to convince myself I'd be content to live without any family or friends for the rest of my existence. I'd grow rich delivering newspapers. I'd be my own boss. I didn't need any damn Mommy or anyone else ever again.

Chapter 38

Emil asked me to go along to the cemetery to visit Naomi's grave. He still didn't understand how much I hated her. Grass had grown over the plot they'd lowered her casket into. All around her, the earth was undisturbed. She hadn't clawed her way up through the black, wormy earth. She couldn't punish me anymore. Emil laid flowers against her three-foot-high marble headstone. The inscription read, "In loving memory, Naomi Johnson, 1894-1954." In loving memory? I didn't have one single loving memory of the beast.

Nearby, people placed flowers on a grave that had a small marble marker flush with the ground. Flowers decorated another grave with an elaborate, ten-foot-high marble statue of Jesus Christ. A marble building adorned with carvings of Jesus and Mother Mary held the remains of a whole family going back a hundred years. As I read the many names of the dead on the different grave markers, I wondered what the people had been like when they were alive. How many had been cruel money-grubbers like Naomi? How many had been poor, but kind people like the colored rag-man, Otis? The life spans carved into the marble monuments ranged from newborn babies to people who'd lived over one-hundred-years. Some had so much life. Too many had very little.

I was back in the alley talking to Otis and petting Horse.

"I visited Naomi's grave," I said.

"Naomi?" Otis looked puzzled.

I forgot I never mentioned Naomi to Otis. "Naomi was the woman I lived with. My real mother left me with her. Naomi had a stroke, died, and was buried. Some people said she went to heaven."

"Heaven is a good place." He gave me a look of sympathy. "How are you feeling about Naomi dying?"

"I can do anything I want now. She's not my boss anymore."

"You didn't like her?"

"No."

"Did you dislike her a lot?"

"I hated her. I thought a lot about killing her."

"Killing her?"

"Well, I thought about it."

"Death is a hard thing," Otis said. "You don't want to be too happy about someone dying. You really don't want to think about killing people."

"She was really cruel. She hit me all the time." I looked down at the better fitting shoes I wore since the beast had died. I got these better shoes because I ran away and caused the monster to have a stroke. Luckily, she died before she could beat me to death. I didn't feel guilty at all about liking the fact she was buried in a cold, dark hole.

"What you going to do now?" Otis asked. Flies swarmed around Horse's eyes, and he stomped his feet. As old and tired as Horse was, he wanted to move on.

"I don't know. I've got my paper routes, and I still have my room, but I don't think Emil wants me to live in his house anymore. He has a new woman, and she doesn't like me one bit."

"Paper routes are good. Things will work out for you, boy."

"Yes, sir. I can take care of myself."

Horse stomped again. He swished his tail at the flies that landed on his scabby back legs.

"I've got to go now, boy. You'll be okay."

"Yeah, I will. I'll be fine. Goodbye, Otis."

"Bye."

Otis and Horse clattered down the alley.

I was glad I could talk to Otis. He listened and talked back to me like I was a real person.

Chapter 39

"Doris called," Emil said. "Her friend Joyce wants you to spend a day with her."

"Joyce?"

"That's what she said. Her friend Joyce."

"Oh, yeah," I said. "I kind of remember her. Why does she want me to spend time with her?"

"I'm not sure, but I think she's considering giving you a home."

"She is. Why would she do that?"

"I don't know. She wants to check you out first. She has money. If you make a good impression on her, she might provide you with a good home and future."

I thought I had a good future delivering newspapers and being free from Naomi. Then, nasty Priscilla showed up at the house and wanted to get rid of me. I didn't want to live with another stranger, but I didn't know how to politely refuse the offer to visit Joyce. I didn't like to disappoint people or make them mad at me.

Joyce arrived early on a Saturday morning driving a big, shiny-black car. I'd been waiting out in front of the house for about an hour.

She rolled down the passenger window after she pulled over to the curb. She leaned over from the driver's seat and said, "Hello, Mickey. Are you ready to go?"

"Yes, ma'am, I'm ready."

I barely remembered meeting Joyce at Doris's house when we left Steve behind five years ago. I climbed into the front seat next to her. She acted friendly like she'd known me for a long time. An older lady and kind of heavy, she wore an expensive looking dress. I looked like a hobo, and I felt terribly out of place in her classy car. Her car looked new and had lots of gadgets, with all kinds of knobs to twist. She told me how close she was to Doris and how much she liked my younger brother, Steve.

"You are quite thin, Mickey. Do you get sick often?"

"No, I don't, ma'am. I'm pretty tough."

"How is school, Mickey?"

"School's okay."

"Do you get good grades?"

"Sometimes, I do. I'm good at reading."

"Do you like sports?"

"I'm really bad at sports. I always get picked last for teams."

"You don't get into trouble, do you?"

"Not anymore, I don't."

"Not anymore?"

"No, ma'am. I don't want to go to prison."

"Why would you go to prison, Mickey?"

"Naomi always said she'd call the cops and have me locked away in a prison if I didn't obey her." I started to feel carsick. My stomach and throat felt like I might puke all over her expensive car. She looked worried and finally quit asking me questions.

I was relieved when we finally arrived in Geneva, and I could get out of the car. Joyce rented a speedboat at a fancy yacht club on the Saint Charles River. She struggled to climb into the boat, but once she was at the controls, she steered confidently. She wasn't as clumsy as she looked.

It was terrific fun speeding around the lake in the sleek boat. The bow rose up to cut through the water, and the bottom slapped against the waves. It felt as if the boat was going to take off and fly. I stuck my hand over the side into the boat's wake and attempted to hold it steady against the pressure of the water, and mostly succeeded.

"Let's try water skiing, Mickey," Joyce said.

We boated past a lot of people who were skimming over the lake's surface on those skinny wooden slats. I couldn't believe they weren't killed when they fell into the water at such high speed.

Joyce gave me new swimming trunks she bought for me. They were way too big for my skinny body, and I was terribly embarrassed when I looked at myself in the changing room mirror. I was terrified by the prospect of standing up on two wood boards and speeding and bouncing across the surface of the big lake. I wasn't only afraid to be injured or drown, I hated being seen in the oversized swimming trunks, and I hated the idea of another athletic failure.

It took many tumbling tries from the shallow water of the shoreline before I stood up on the water skis. Joyce was growing impatient. I was sure I'd break both my legs and drown, but drowning would be better than failing her test. My spindly legs and lack of coordination were too obvious. My entire pale, skinny body was exposed by the too big, and now soaking wet, pair of swim trunks. I feared the trunks would slide down my bony legs and expose me completely.

I was glad when Joyce gave up hope I'd be a water skier. Mercifully, she let me get back into the boat. I was shivering, and my teeth chattered from the cold water. I pulled on the oversized tee shirt she also bought for me. I prayed I wouldn't ever have to try that crazy, water skiing crap again. Disappointment showed clearly on Joyce's face.

We ate lunch on the patio of a fancy lakeside restaurant. I wolfed down a big, delicious cheeseburger. I made sure to use a napkin to wipe my mouth rather than the back of my hand. I hoped I'd finally made a good impression on Joyce.

"I have two paper routes, and I make lots of money," I bragged. "The bosses say I'm really good."

"That's impressive, Mickey."

"I go wherever I want to go and stay out as late as I want to."

"Really, Mickey?"

"Yes, ma'am."

Joyce didn't appear terribly impressed by my lifestyle or my bragging. I gave up on telling her about my exciting life on the streets of Chicago.

After lunch, we drove to the small local airport, where Joyce introduced me to a male friend of hers. Tall, thin and balding, Oliver owned a two-seater plane.

"Would you like to go up in my plane, Mickey," he asked me as he shook my hand. His hand was clammy and limp.

The thought of flying scared me. "I've never flown in a plane before, sir."

"It'll be exciting," Oliver said. "I'm a good pilot."

I climbed into the passenger seat as he flipped switches and turned knobs. "Have fun, Mickey," Joyce said cheerfully as she waved us off. "Take good care of him, Oliver."

Oliver reached over to check how tight I had my seatbelt. The touch of his hand so close to my privates made me flinch. I didn't trust any person's hands coming near me in any way, let alone close to my crotch. He looked and moved more like the men who lurked in Garfield Park than one of the heroic pilots from the war movies.

We taxied to the main runway. The plane vibrated and got real noisy as we picked up speed. It lifted slightly into the air, then bumped back onto the blacktop. I tensed my whole body for the crash. The plane lifted again. We rose up away from the ground. I took a big breath. I was grateful to still be alive. We climbed higher and higher. The plane bounced around in the air currents. I tried to relax and enjoy flying. Oliver pushed the steering wheel forward, and we leveled out. Directly ahead of us loomed a mountainous cloud. We flew directly into the grey mass. Again, I feared the end of my life was near. But the plane burst out of the mist and into a brilliant, blue sky. The earth spread out before us.

Oliver turned and smiled at me.

"Hang on Mickey," he shouted. "This will be fun."

During a wide, forty-five-degree turn downward towards the earth, a strange force pressed me back into my seat. Flying in this plane reminded me of a wild roller coaster ride at an amusement park, except there wasn't a lot of chattering noise and ups and downs, and the turns weren't quite as jarring.

We climbed back up towards heaven. We flew through another layer of misty clouds. After we were clear of those clouds, Oliver pushed a knob and the engine shut off. The sudden quiet was eerie. He pushed forward on the steering wheel. We glided silently towards the earth. The vast landscape below us looked like a green, brown and blue patchwork quilt. The plane picked up speed. Faster and faster we went as we approached the ground. I clearly saw roads with cars traveling along them. I held my breath. Was something wrong with the plane? Oliver took one hand off the steering wheel. He pulled a knob. The engine sputtered a couple of times, and finally, roared back to life. He pulled back on the steering wheel with both hands. We leveled out. Jesus! My stomach went up in my throat.

Oliver reached over and placed his hand on my thigh. He squeezed. I felt a terrible fear that he'd touch my penis.

"Had you a little scared there, didn't I Mickey? No need to worry. I do that a lot. The engine always restarts."

The nausea I felt from his touching my leg so close to my privates was worse than my nausea from the flying. I pressed against the thin-metal passenger door. Thoughts of that door flipping open, and me falling thousands of feet to the ground flooded my mind. I'd end up dead in one of the fields far below us. I'd smash into the hard earth and end up as a bloody blotch in a cornfield. Those images scared me almost as much as Oliver putting his hands on me.

"We're going to land now, Mickey."

I wanted to be brave and keep my eyes open during the landing, and I somewhat did. Mainly, I tensed my body really tight and held my breath as we grew closer and closer to the ground. The wheels screeched against the asphalt. The plane bounced back up into the air. I was sure I was going to die in a fiery crash and be burned into tiny cinders that would float away in a breeze. We touched down again and stayed on the runway. As the plane slowed down, I relaxed.

With the plane safely on the ground, Oliver reached over and gripped my shoulder. He squeezed, and it didn't seem like he'd ever let go. I tensed up again from his touching me. I ungratefully thought, God, get me out of this plane and away from him.

"Thanks, sir. That flying was great fun."

"It's Oliver, Mickey."

I hoped I hadn't hurt his feelings. Maybe, I misjudged him; I couldn't tell for sure what his intentions were.

After we taxied back to the hanger, Joyce greeted us with a big smile, but I was sure she noticed everything wasn't perfect between Oliver and me.

I was totally exhausted by the time Joyce drove me home. I fell asleep during the trip. When she woke me up, we were parked in front of Emil's house.

"Thanks for spending the day with me, Mickey."

"Thank you, ma'am. I had lots of fun."

"So did I, Mickey. Goodbye now."

I climbed out of her car. I stood on the sidewalk and waved as she drove away.

I went over the day's events in my mind. I was sure I'd failed her test. I'd been awful at water skiing. And, I was sure she realized I didn't like Oliver. What the hell was wrong with me? Why couldn't I ever be what people wanted me to be? Jesus Christ. Joyce wasn't going to want me to live with her, let alone adopt me.

I trudged up the steps to the front door. Damn. I wasn't crazy about the idea of living with her anyway. She acted pleasant, but she was another stranger I didn't trust. Wearily, I climbed the stairway up to my room. As I entered my cave of solitude, I remembered what was good in my life. The monster, Naomi, was dead, she was buried, and it didn't look like she'd rise from the dead. I felt better. I didn't need anyone in this world except myself.

Chapter 40

I ran into creepy Eric in the park again. He smiled at me and said hello like I was a long lost friend. He sat next to me on my park bench and talked at me. I hadn't conversed with a grownup this much before. In my life filled with solitude and mistrust, I had very few people to talk to.

"You're a lovely boy, Mickey. You should have a much better life than you do."

I didn't want to hurt his feelings, so I finally let him buy me dinner.

Eric requested a booth in the very back corner of the diner. People stared at us as we walked past them. I was embarrassed about my street-urchin clothes and my messy haircut. I wondered what the other diners thought of a poorly-dressed, twelve-year-old, blonde-haired boy and a fastidiously attired and balding, older man sharing a meal. We certainly didn't look like a loving father and his happy son spending time together.

Eric fiddled nervously, and our cranky waitress didn't smile. Still, I liked the bright chrome, the black and white plastic booths, and the black and white tiles on the floor. The overhead lights reflected off the shiny, chrome milkshake mixer, and the chrome spinner the orders were clipped to.

"I'd like something different than a hamburger, sir," I said.

"Have whatever you want, Mickey," Eric replied generously. "You can order anything on the menu that suits your fancy."

"Thanks, sir."

I ordered a hot roast beef sandwich and a glass of Coca-Cola.

While we waited for our food, Eric asked me a lot of hard-to-answer grownup questions about what I did and what I liked. My life as an abandoned, unwanted kid wasn't anything I wanted to talk about, and I didn't tell him much.

I was glad when our waitress brought our food. My meal was served on a big plate, and it looked really delicious. Dark gravy covered a generous portion of roast beef between two slices of white bread, and there was a big mound of mashed potatoes, also covered with brown gravy.

Eric had a cup of coffee and a boring, corned beef on rye sandwich.

He watched me eat.

I ate so fast I couldn't talk to Eric. I took big gulps from my tall glass of cola. Eric ate slowly and watched me even more. I wished he wouldn't stare at me the way he did. He looked at me as if I was some kind of zoo animal in a cage. He made me really nervous.

It had turned dark by the time we finished eating and left the diner. My stomach was full, and I was feeling good, but I was worrying about how I could politely get away from Eric. Because of my damn worn-thin, oversized clothes, I shivered as we walked down the street.

"Come up to my place for dessert, Mickey," Eric invited me. "We'll have milk and cookies."

"Oh no, sir. I really shouldn't."

"It'll be okay, Mickey." I'd hurt his feelings again. I hated that look. I didn't want to be rude and run off after the great meal he bought for me.

"Okay, sir. But, I have to be home soon."

I'd just told a big, fat lie. I didn't really have a home like regular kids. Emil didn't care what time I showed up at his house. I was sure he'd be happy if I totally disappeared from his life.

Eric lived in a six-story, brick apartment building that had a fancy entry door and a small, but high-class lobby. We took the elevator up four floors. I stood as far away from Eric as I could. Damn. I offended him again.

He brushed against me as we left the elevator. I moved away from him, but he kept moving close to me. I hate when people do that.

He unlocked and opened the door to his apartment. With a sweep of his hand, he motioned for me to enter first. The lights in his small flat were dim. I hoped he'd turn them up brighter, but he didn't.

"I'll get the cookies, Mickey."

I sat on his couch. His furniture was dark-wood stuff, and his place was painfully neat. He came out of the kitchen and placed a plate of butter cookies, one of my favorites, on the coffee table in front of me.

"Darn it. I'm sorry, Mickey, but I'm out of milk." Eric sounded like he was really sorry he was out of milk.

I'd already eaten one cookie and started on a second.

"Here, Mickey. This is good to drink."

He poured something from a thick, dark bottle into a glass and handed it to me. I took a drink. The liquid was orange, syrupy and bitter, but it helped the cookies down. I drank more of the sticky stuff so Eric wouldn't get that offended look on his face again. I ate more butter cookies and drank more orange syrup. My mouth turned gummy. I felt good, but I was kind of dizzy and sleepy and felt strange. My world went black.

The lights were still dim when I woke up. My head ached. I'd eaten too many cookies and drank too much of the orange syrup stuff. My mouth felt like it was packed full of cotton. I struggled to focus my eyes. I saw someone sitting across from me. I remembered him. It was Eric. He sat stiff and upright in his chair with his hands in front of his face in a little tent posture. He stared at me, and the expression on his face was less friendly than it was in the park and at the diner. I felt sick like I needed to puke. My clothes didn't feel right. I adjusted my oversized pants as I stood up. I almost fell over from dizziness.

"I have to go, sir." My voice was all mumbly.

"Okay, Mickey. I'll walk you down to the street."

Eric didn't try to be close to me now.

I felt huge relief he didn't crowd me anymore.

The lights in the hallway were much brighter than those in Eric's apartment. My eyes struggled to adjust.

The sudden downward plunge of the elevator pushed me closer to puking.

He walked me halfway up the block.

"Goodnight, Mickey. I'll see you in the park."

"Sure, sir."

The night was shivery cold, foggy wet, and scary dark. I walked and ran towards Emil's house. I passed dark doorways, dark recesses, and dark alleys.

Breathy, raspy voices whispered loudly, "Good morning, son."

I moved closer to the gutter. I ran faster. A sour taste surged in my throat and mouth. I stopped and bent over. I threw up. God, it feels awful to puke. I wiped my lips with my overlong shirtsleeve.

After forever, I reached the house. I still felt panicky. I ran up the front steps. I fumbled with the key as I unlocked the front door. I hurriedly stepped through the vestibule and raced up the stairway. I slammed the door shut behind me. Still dressed, I crawled under the covers.

I didn't ever want to leave the safety of my bed again.

"I'LL SEE YOU IN THE PARK, MICKEY!"

Chapter 41

I stayed away from the park and the creeps that wandered there, and my world looked better. I had my own money from my paper routes to spend any way I wanted to. I bought comic books, and I traded with a kid my age that lived down the block from the house. Jeremy wore nice clothes, but he was a nervous kid who blinked too much and constantly rubbed a finger under his nose. He wasn't as weird as me, but not many kids liked him. I hoped he hadn't gotten too much of his snot on the comic books

"How were you able to sneak away from that big woman who keeps you as a prisoner in her house?" he asked.

"I didn't have to sneak. The fat cow is dead."

"That terrible woman is dead? You're not her prisoner anymore?"

"No, I'm not her prisoner anymore. I'm free to do whatever I want."

"How did she die?"

"She was beating me with her broomstick and she dropped dead from a heart attack."

"So you killed her?"

"Yeah, I killed her."

"How did it feel to kill someone?"

"The real truth is I ran away, the coppers caught me, and she had a stroke in the middle of that night. After a while, she died. I saw her lying dead in her fancy casket during her funeral. I saw them close the lid on her casket and seal it shut. I saw them lower her casket into a deep hole in the cemetery, and I watched them cover her casket with shovelfuls of earth. I don't think she'll ever rise up from the dead like Jesus did."

"She might be in heaven, waiting for you."

"She might be. Shit. Maybe, I won't ever be able to escape from her."

Korean War comic books were my favorite reading material. I imagined being a heavily-muscled soldier, exhaling big clouds of smoke from the Camel cigarette I clenched tightly between my lips, as I blasted the charging gooks with a machine gun.

Jeremy liked them too, and we were sort of friends.

"How about you come over to my place for lunch, Mickey."

"You sure that'll be okay?"

"Yeah. My dad's at work and my mom doesn't live with us anymore."

He lived in a nice second-floor apartment. We raided his refrigerator and made big sandwiches.

Mine was a white-bread sandwich with three slices of luncheon meat, two slices of American cheese and mustard. Jeremy copied me but used mayonnaise.

"My dad fought in World War Two against the Japs. He has medals, and a Jap sword, and lots of guns in his room, but I'm not allowed in there when he's not at home."

"I'd love to see that kind of stuff."

"We could sneak a look, but don't ever tell anyone."

"I never tattle-tale about anything."

His dad's room was filled with amazing treasures. The sword hung on the wall along with a Japanese flag, combat medals, and photos of dead Japanese soldiers. Rifles stood in gun racks, pistols lay neatly organized on a table, and hundreds of rounds of ammo were stacked everywhere. I really wanted to pick up and feel the guns in my hands. The photos of the dead Japs were both sickening and fascinating."

Jeremy looked really proud he could show off his Dad's stuff.

I'd almost picked up a pistol when I heard the door to his apartment open. After a few loud footsteps, a large man appeared in the doorway.

A frightened Jeremy said, "This is my friend Mickey, Dad."

"What have I told you, Jeremy? Your friend better leave now."

I scooted past him out of the room and towards the apartment door. I heard the lash of a belt and a cry from Jeremy, "I'm sorry, Dad."

As I hustled down the stairs, I heard another lash and yelp of pain.

I was halfway out the front door when I heard Jeremy cry out again. Goddamn.

I had a good collection of marbles I bought. I played marbles a few times with other kids, but I got tired of losing. It's a tough game to master, and I was way behind, in those kinds of physical skills, compared to most of the kids my age. I bought more marbles just to have them.

I was sure Priscilla's big bully of a son Curtis searched my room often, so I was really careful with my money. I exercised extreme caution when I entered the room. I didn't want the fat slob to trap me in such a small space and beat me to a bloody pulp. I always wanted to make sure I had room to escape.

Lots of the time, I bought my own food. At times I was able to avoid Priscilla and Curtis and eat food from the house.

When I attended the movies, I didn't care that I looked like a poor, street bum. The people lined up to see the movies were mostly well-dressed adult couples. The pretty young women who sold me my tickets usually gave me looks of surprise. That was okay. I paid with money I earned working my paper routes. My own money!

I usually pushed my way through the crowd in the theatre lobby and up to the concession counter. I bought a large popcorn with butter, a big box of jujubees, and a large soda. With my wonderful movie goodies in hand, I found a seat in the middle of the crowded theatre. Cologne-scented, cigarette-puffing moviegoers surrounded me. I admired the pretty women in the audience, and I imagined one of them would adopt me and take me home. But there wasn't any chance of that happening to someone like me. I felt like a boy from Mars dropped into this world where I was mostly ignored. The fancy evening theatre showings were a huge change from the raucous movie matinees I'd gone to with my older brothers, back when I was a rowdy, little kid.

A film about French Legionnaires fighting hordes of fanatical natives of India, who worshipped evil spirits that appeared out of clouds of smoke, made me want to be a good guy swinging a sword. I didn't want to be sliced in half by one of those super-sharp, curved swords the crazy, turbaned Indians used. Jesus. Being sliced up by a sharp blade must be the worst way to die.

I remembered Jeremy and the Jap soldier sword hung on his father's bedroom wall and the photos of dead Japanese soldiers. Worst of all, I recalled Jeremy's father beating him with a belt. Naomi didn't seem so bad compared to that big and angry ex-marine. I was lucky not to have a father, and I hated the thought of ever having another stepfather.

I ran into Jeremy again. His eyes were still blinking, and he was rubbing his finger under his nose more rapidly.

"What was it like when you ran away from the woman you lived with, Mickey?"

"It was great at first, but then I realized I didn't have anywhere to go to escape from Naomi. I didn't have food or water, and I was afraid to get a ride from a stranger. I think I'd have figured something out if the copper hadn't picked me up."

"When I run away from my dad, I'm going to take food and water and a blanket. If I knew where my mother lived now, I'd find her."

"Be careful, Jeremy."

"Maybe I'll load one of my Dad's guns and shoot him."

"Jesus Christ. Don't miss. He might kill you."

"I'll shoot him while he's asleep. I could use the Samurai sword to chop off his head. I don't know if I'm strong enough, and I don't know how brave I'll be. He always says I'm a little wimp."

"Maybe it's better if you just run away, Jeremy. I don't know where my mother is either. We're both in the same rotten boat."

Chapter 42

One day, when I walked into the house, Emil was sitting at the dining room table waiting for me to show up.

"Mickey. I have something important to tell you."

"You do?" Dread engulfed me.

"Yes. I located your mother and talked to her."

Excitement surged through me. "My mother? You talked to my mother? Where is she?"

"She's living in Ogden, Utah with her new husband and his daughter," he said. "She wasn't overjoyed to hear from me. She told me she doesn't want you back. She said she doesn't have room for you. I couldn't believe what your worthless mother said. She's supposed to be raising you! You're her son."

My guts twisted into a tight knot. Mom had said she didn't want me back? How could that be true? Didn't she care one tiny bit about me? Didn't she worry I might die, and she wouldn't ever see me again?

"I told her I'd get the law after her if she didn't take you back," Emil said.

I tried to form a reply, but Emil continued.

"I can't keep you, Mickey." Emil's voice betrayed a rare anger. "Your new stepfather works for the Union Pacific railroad. They're going to send a train ticket. Then you'll leave for Utah."

"Where is Utah?" I wanted to puke.

"Utah is out west, a long ways from Chicago."

"When do I leave?"

"You'll return to your mother soon, I think."

Oh God! Sour crud rose in my throat. I didn't want another mean stepfather like the cabbie Roy that Mom had been married to for a short while. I was always afraid of him. I was glad I didn't have any kind of father anymore. I was satisfied with the way my life was now. I was my own boss.

I was terrified by the thought of a reunion with my mother. She said she didn't want me back? Now, I knew for sure she didn't love me. How should I act when I saw her again? What would I say to her?

My train ticket arrived. It was time for me to leave Chicago and travel to a strange place called Utah. Emil and I took a cab to the train depot. Neither of us talked during the ride. At least, I now knew there wasn't any reason to look for Mom among the people who walked the city streets. After she gave me to Naomi to be a slave, Mom had gone out to the Wild West. She'd found a new husband, and she had a new family.

If Mom really loved me, she'd have kept me. If she'd taken me out West with her, I'd be a tough, bronco-riding cowboy by now. Damn her to hell!

The train station was crowded with people rushing around in a hurry and as noisy and entertaining as an amusement park. The excitement momentarily distracted me from my anger and fear.

All around me powerful locomotives shot outbursts of steam, and shiny aluminum passenger cars awaited travelers going to the exotic destinations the uniformed conductors called out. I was at the beginning of an exciting and glamorous train journey. Now, I didn't feel so sad.

"Rock Island and Des Moines, Iowa," sang out the conductor of the train I would board. "Omaha. Columbus. Grand Island and North Platte, Nebraska."

He continued to sing out his list of magical cities of the great American Plains and Wild West. "Cheyenne, Laramie, Rawlins, Bitter Creek and Evanston, Wyoming. Wasatch and Ogden, Utah."

Ogden, Utah. That's where I was going. It sounded like a magical land where I'd enjoy thrilling cowboy adventures. But there was a terrifying reunion waiting for me in Ogden.

"All aboard!"

The wonderful neighbor, Anna, who'd been a nurse to Naomi and a good friend to me had given me a warm goodbye hug and handed me a package of fried chicken to take on my big train trip. I carried that, along with a paper bag containing my comic books, my marbles, my extra pair of undershorts and my extra pair of matching socks.

The conductor who punched a hole in my ticket said, "Welcome aboard our train, Mr. Mickey Shafer."

"Thank you, sir." I smiled up at him.

I was surprised by his words. Then, I remembered. It was my real name he read from my ticket. I forgot my real last name was Shafer. I'd been Mickey Johnson for four, long, dark, brutal years.

I turned to Emil. "Good-bye, Emil."

"Good-bye," he said. "You'll be okay, boy." Emil had called me boy. I guessed he didn't want to say my name. He didn't look either sad or happy I was leaving him.

I couldn't think of anything else to say.

Emil didn't offer to shake my hand.

I clambered up the metal steps of the train car.

I entered the fancy looking car. There were only a few other passengers aboard. I picked out a good window seat. Through the thick glass, I watched Emil walk away. I didn't know if I'd ever see or talk to him again. He hadn't ever yelled at me, hit me or tried to touch my privates. After Naomi died, he let me do whatever I wanted to do. But I now knew he always intended to get rid of me. I waved goodbye to him, but he didn't turn around to wave goodbye to me. He walked away as if I never mattered. The way Emil acted made me terribly sad.

The train shuddered and lurched forward. I was on my way to a new life.

Damn. I wasn't Mickey Johnson anymore. Naomi was dead and buried and didn't own me anymore. I wasn't her slave. Mickey Johnson, the slave, was gone forever. I was Mickey Shafer again. This new world I was traveling to might be the wonderful place I always hoped for. I was on my way to a much better life. Damn.

THE END

Past Titles

Running Wild Stories Anthology, Volume 1

Running Wild Anthology of Novellas, Volume 1

Jersey Diner by Lisa Diane Kastner

Magic Forgotten by Jack Hillman

The Kidnapped by Dwight L. Wilson

Running Wild Stories Anthology, Volume 2

Running Wild Novella Anthology, Volume 2, Part 1

Running Wild Novella Anthology, Volume 2, Part 2

Running Wild's Best of 2017, AWP Special Edition

Build Your Music Career From Scratch, Second Edition by Andrae Alexander

Writers Resist: Anthology 2018 with featured editors Sara Marchant and Kit-Bacon Gressitt

Magic Forbidden by Jack Hillman

Frontal Matter: Glue Gone Wild by Suzanne Samples

Upcoming Titles

Running Wild Press, Best of 2018
Dark Corners by Reuben Tihi Hayslett
Running Wild Stories Anthology, Volume 3
Running Wild Stories Anthology, Volume 4
Open My Eyes by Tommy Hahn
Legendary by Amelia Kibbie
Running Wild Novella Anthology, Volume 3
Running Wild Novella Anthology, Volume 4
Christine, Released by E. Burke
The Resistors by Dwight L. Wilson

Running Wild Press publishes stories that don't fit neatly in a box. Our team consists of:

Lisa Diane Kastner, Founder and Executive Editor
Barbara Lockwood, Editor
Cecile Serruf, Editor
Jenna Faccenda, Public Relations
Rachael Angelo, Public Relations
Tone Milazzo, Podcast Interviewer Extraordinaire
Amrita Raman, Project Manager
Lisa Montagne, Director of Education

Learn more about us and our stories at www.runningwildpress.com

Loved this story and want more? Follow us at
www.runningwildpress.com, www.facebook.com/runningwildpress, on
Twitter @lisadkastner @JadeBlackwater @RunWildBooks

CPSIA information can be obtained
at www.ICGtesting.com
Printed in the USA
FSHW011255200619
59261FS